This is ~ — tory
that is so incredible
and inspiring

Saint Magnus
The Last Viking

♡
Melissa,
Danika,
Angeline

Other books by Susan Peek:

Crusader King
A Soldier Surrenders

Watch for more titles in her exciting new series:

"God's Forgotten Friends"

Saint Magnus
The Last Viking

Susan Peek

Cover design by Theresa Linden

ISBN 13: 978-0-9970005-0-4 by Seven Swords Publications
ISBN 10: 0997000503 by Seven Swords Publications

Previous edition ISBN 978-0-9796301-2-5 Catholic Vitality Publications 2014

For ordering information contact:

SevenSwordsPublications@gmail.com

www.susanpeekauthor.com

"In many chapels,

reddened by the setting sun,

the saints rest silently,

waiting for someone to love them."

These words, penned by an unknown priest, long dead, were the inspiration for this series on the lives of saints who have fallen deep into the shadows of obscurity. My hope is that, in reading their heroic stories, you will make the acquaintance of some of

God's Forgotten Friends

Susan Peek

My sincerest gratitude to the Benedictine Monks of Our Lady of Guadalupe Monastery, Silver City, New Mexico, for their overwhelming kindness in reading and helping edit my manuscript.

To my wonderful friend and fellow author of the Catholic Writers' Guild, Theresa Linden: Thank you so much for your assistance, encouragement, and tremendous inspiration. You are not only a true friend, but the best author I know! May God bless you always!

And last, but never least, I thank my loving husband Jeff, who has been behind me every step of the way. Not only has he patiently put up with an author for a wife, but he taught me nearly everything I know about writing. I could never have done this without him!

To Our Lady Queen of Peace,

and to Saint Magnus, of course,

with the prayer that he will find

"someone to love him."

Chapter One

(The Orkney Islands, North of Scotland, 1065)

The old warrior lay dying. Thorfinn the Mighty they'd called him in life, but stretched as he was upon this bed of anguish the aged Jarl felt anything but full of the vigor his name implied. Gone forever, he knew, were the days of his youth and valor, useless now and devoid of power was the jeweled crown which had adorned his brow, empty the throne he had occupied for so many years. There was only one job left for Thorfinn the Mighty to do, after which he could finally die.

His eyesight was failing, but he knew his bedchamber was crowded. Physicians, thralls, Chieftains, and no doubt more than one curious onlooker had gathered to watch their ruler's passing. He could feel Ingibjorg holding his cold hand in the warmth of her own as she sat on the bed beside him. Faithful and loving she was to the end, and Thorfinn was grateful God had blessed him with such a Christian wife. But there was not the time, nor had Thorfinn the breath, to speak to her now; he had but one matter left to address, and the words would not be for Ingibjorg, but for the two she had borne him.

He spoke; his strained voice came out not more than a whisper. "Paal. Erlend. My sons, come forth."

"We are here, Father. Right beside you." It would, of course, be Erlend who answered. The younger one. The better one. Thorfinn's favorite. Oh, Paal was a good son too. Good, but, alas, very weak. Not a man to rule a kingdom. Unfortunately, Paal was the rightful heir, the eldest. But Erlend, his father knew, was the more deserving.

The old Jarl drew a ragged breath. These thoughts --- about his two sons, his throne, and who should henceforth sit upon it --- had tormented him ever since he'd found out he was dying. He had dwelt upon almost nothing else in these pain-filled days, and now, at long last, he had made his decision. He knew what he had to do, for the welfare of the Orkney Kingdom.

He spoke, his voice still firm despite his feebleness. "I call on God and the Chieftains here to witness. I wish to change my Will."

He felt, rather than actually saw, the astonishment which flickered across every face. The gathering of men fell silent. Tense. Even Ingibjorg's hand seemed to ice over, suddenly as cold as his own. For a king to alter his Will at the hour of death was, understandably, an unpleasant surprise to spring upon anyone. Especially upon those subjects whose personal fortunes were suddenly at stake.

But Thorfinn felt he had no choice.

His dimming eyes rested upon the face of his eldest son. "Paal," he began, "you are my firstborn and therefore my heir. I bequeath to you the whole of my kingdom, which is yours by birthright. Rule it with justice and mercy till the day you shall die."

He saw Paal breathe an infinitesimal sigh of relief. No surprises here. "Yes, of course, Father. You know I will."

A few quirky eyebrows were raised around the room. This wasn't the altering of a Will. Ingibjorg's hand relaxed again.

But the Jarl wasn't finished.

Thorfinn shifted his steady gaze to his youngest, and delivered the stroke which he knew would rock half of Scandinavia.

"And you, Erlend, my second-born . . . I bequeath to you also the whole of my kingdom, to reign together with your brother. Your power shall be equal to his in all things, and henceforth no one shall dispute you as their rightful Jarl."

Thorfinn's words blasted a shockwave through the room. *What? Two heirs to the same throne! Why, this was unheard of! Impossible! Had the Mighty lost his mind?*

There was, as he expected there would be, a horrified silence, which swiftly gave way to an outpouring of objections. The chamber exploded into a chaos of noise and murmurs, shocked and angry voices volleying back and forth, everyone suddenly talking at once. The dying Jarl felt as if he were being clobbered.

But he bravely ignored it all. His eyes and his attention were locked upon only two men, Paal and Erlend, and he noticed that they alone, of everyone in the room, remained motionless and deathly silent.

Then, slowly, the two brothers exchanged between themselves a bewildered yet sympathetic look, as if their beloved father had gone mad before their very eyes, and in that second Thorfinn knew he had indeed done the right thing. For, strange as it was, it was precisely that shared look of compassion between them that the Jarl had wildly hoped to see, and his heart beat in secret peace. His boys had, in that split-second gaze, turned instinctively to each other --- not against each other --- when faced with their father's apparent insanity and the most fateful twist of their lives. Well, if they could face *that* together, surely they could face anything.

Perhaps Thorfinn chose rightly; perhaps he chose wrongly.

But he couldn't see the future.

"All here are my witnesses," he went on, the authority in his voice quelling the room's storm. "As of this day, my two sons, Paal and Erlend, shall reign as one, and both their eldest sons shall likewise reign as one after them. And their eldest sons, and their eldest, and in this way shall my line continue for as long as this kingdom shall be."

No one moved, as the king's incredible proclamation was digested.

Exhausted now, Thorfinn closed his tired eyes and breathed in peace.

Little did he who was called the Mighty realize what violence --- and what sanctity --- his dying decision would breed amongst his grandsons yet unborn . . .

Chapter Two

(Twenty-six years later, 1091)

It had never occurred to Magnus, second son of Erlend, to arm himself with a weapon before setting off for Vespers. Why should it, after all? The church was but a few miles' walk from his father's fortress and the surrounding countryside was plenty safe enough. No outlaws dared lurk in these parts; his father and Uncle Paal, the two ruling Jarls, made certain of that. Their combined power was absolute, their justice swift and fierce, and the people bowed to their laws. Thus, it did not even cross the young man's mind to carry a sword to attend the church's evening prayers.

Even when Magnus first spotted the thin column of smoke rising through the distant trees, he wasn't alarmed. The air was turning brisk and it was only normal that fires would be kindled upon the farmhouse hearths. From his position on the high path he could easily guess which dwelling the smoke was coming from. There was only one farm in the clearing over there, that of the widower, Helge Stianson. Magnus knew the abode well. How could he not? His older brother Aerling had in recent weeks taken an avid interest in Helge's lovely daughter Grida, and rumors already ran rampart that she would someday be the wife of one of the next two Jarls. Magnus would believe it when he saw it. It was natural, of course, that his older brother would eventually choose a bride, but, knowing Aerling, he would put off tying himself down for as long as possible. After all, he was one of the two crown-princes and every unwed daughter of every Chieftain in the kingdom was after him. Aerling certainly would not be choosing amongst them in a hurry.

Still, in the meantime, Magnus couldn't help but be amused that his hot-headed warrior brother could turn to mush at the mere name of Helge's sweet and graceful daughter. But that's exactly the effect Grida had on him at the moment. Her very presence made him melt, steel armor and all. Yet in order to tease Aerling about anything --- Grida or otherwise --- one either had to know him extremely well, or be suicidal, because it was something you just didn't do. Not if you valued life and limb. But Magnus got away with it. He was the only one in the kingdom; no one else would dare. Which is why he found it so entertaining these last few weeks to see how easily Grida could make Aerling fall apart the way she did. It was spectacular to watch, and what younger brother in the world could resist a little provocation every now and then, even at the risk of premature death? It was just too good to pass up.

"You don't know anything. You're hardly more than a newborn colt," was one of Aerling's typical replies. "Just wait till you're older and you'll start noticing the Chieftains' daughters too. Take my word for it."

Well sorry, but seventeen wasn't exactly a newborn and Magnus was already noticing the girls. Every single one of them. There were plenty of young things with their eyes on him too, and they made no secret about it. But Magnus hoped against hope that he would someday be allowed to enter the Eynhallow Monastery and give his life to One Who was infinitely more worthy of his love than any pretty girl on the Isles. Yet he could only enter if he managed to obtain the permission and blessing of his father, Jarl

Erlend, without which he would not go. And that, unfortunately, was proving to be much easier said than done. The answer was firmly and irrevocably *no,* and Magnus somehow felt sure that God did not want him to go against his father's wishes. God must have other plans for him, plans which he did not yet know.

He let out a resigned sigh. Oh how much simpler life would have been, he mused as he walked along, if he had been born of lower blood. But he was a prince, a grandson of Thorfinn the Mighty and son of one of the two reigning Jarls. Of course Aerling, not he, was their father's heir and next in line for the Orkney throne, jointly with their cousin Hakon, the only son of Jarl Paal. They were the two future kings. Yet the notion of Magnus hiding away his young life behind cloister walls was most disagreeable to Jarl Erlend, and Magnus saw in his father's decision the holy Will of God. So accept it he would; which didn't mean it wasn't painful.

These thoughts of Eynhallow Monastery and his inability to enter tugged his mind back to the present. Vespers at the church, that was where he was heading and if he didn't hurry he was going to be late. He quickened his pace along the path. And that's when he heard the first screams.

"Help! Help me!" The far-off cry carried on the evening breeze.

Startled, Magnus stopped in his tracks and listened.

After a moment it came again, the voice of a female, and she sounded terrified.

"Save me! Someone please!"

With a shock, Magnus realized that the frantic cries were coming from the direction of Helge Stianson's hut. Grida! It had to be her. . .who else? To his alarm he suddenly noticed that while he had been daydreaming about the monastery, what had moments earlier been but a thin stream of distant smoke from the farmstead had somehow turned into a nightmarish black cloud, billowing high above the clearing. He realized with horror that Helge's entire house must be on fire. And Grida was trapped!

Not stopping to consider what he was going to do about it, Magnus broke into a run toward the dwelling. The first flickering of fear gripped him as he remembered that Helge was not at home with his daughter. Magnus had just seen him, not fifteen minutes ago, at his own father's fortress, which meant that Grida was down there alone. Would he get to her in time? Would he even be able to find her in the inferno? The hellish smoke was rising higher every second. He barged his way through the rough woods, oblivious to the sharp branches that reached out to snag him, aware only that he must rescue Grida.

"Save me! Please help me!"

Grida's wild screams were closer now, and louder. At least she was still alive.

"I beg you, for the love of God, let me go!"

What on. . .earth? What had Magnus just heard? *Let me go?*

As if to verify the strange words, Grida cried out again, "Let go of me! Please! I'm begging you!" Her voice was hysterical.

The meaning of what she was saying struck Magnus in full force. For an instant he hesitated, mind racing. Grida was not alone after all. She was being attacked. But. . .by whom? How many? What was happening? He had no way of knowing, and here he was, completely unarmed and alone. He had certainly never dreamed he would need a sword for a gentle evening's stroll to Vespers. So now what?

Magnus knew he had only two choices. He could either continue to plow through the trees to the farmstead and try to face the situation alone, or he could run for more help. But where? There was no one else out here, and the fortress was over a mile away.

Magnus's decision was made in an instant. Whatever was going on down there, Grida needed rescuing very quickly. He might have no weapon, no plan, no back-up, but he had God, and that was plenty.

Putting aside any fear, Magnus crashed through the last of the woods and onto the edge of the clearing. He stopped and tried to take in the appalling scene of destruction before him. That the widower's homestead could not be saved was immediately apparent. The blaze was completely out of control. But the widower's daughter? Could Magnus still save her?

Magnus's eyes were already starting to sting from the black smoke; the fire's heat lashed out at him furiously even from this distance. He strained to see through the terrifying haze. Grida's screaming had abruptly stopped, which was not a good sign. The only sounds now were the eerie lapping of the flames and Magnus's own ragged breathing. *Grida*, he pleaded in his heart, *where are you?*

A horse's whinny suddenly broke the silence and Magnus spotted a commotion in a clump of trees. Mounts. Four of them. They were spooked by the fire and trying to get away. One man, his face hidden by a mask, was fighting to control them. The horses were tied, but, even so, the man's job was not easy. He obviously had his hands full attempting to keep the animals calm.

Only four, Magnus thought to himself. Well, it could be worse. If only he had a weapon.

Never mind. He had something nearly as good. . .the element of surprise. The man in the mask had not seen him.

Magnus backed up into the woods again and looked for something – anything – that could be used to advantage. A large rock was the only thing he could find. He picked it up and was pleased by its weight. There was a slight incline of land behind the horses . . . If he could sneak up there undetected, he would have the perfect place to launch his missile.

Stealthily he made his way to the small knoll directly above the trees where the frantic animals were tied. They were stomping and snorting; the handler had all he could do to keep them from breaking free. He was distracted and completely off-guard; this was going to be so easy it was almost ridiculous. Magnus positioned himself quietly above his unsuspecting victim, heaved the huge rock over his head, and thrust it with all his might.

His aim was perfect. With a sickening thud the rock hit the man's skull, and he collapsed limply in the dirt.

One down, three to go.

Magnus scrambled down the slope and swiftly found the unconscious man's dagger. It wasn't much; he had hoped for a sword, but this was better than nothing. There was no time to waste. Where was Grida?

Hastily loosing three of the horses, which galloped away in panic, Magnus jumped onto the back of the fourth. It reared wildly, trying also to escape. He held on tight and looked around.

Over there! In the distance another masked figure was running, his arms laden with Helge's few measly treasures, which he greedily clutched as he stumbled away from the burning hut. Magnus charged the horse towards him. The startled thief saw him coming and turned to flee. In his alarm to get out of the steed's way, he dumped the plunder and ran for his life.

It was tempting to pursue him, but all that mattered right now was Grida.

The horse, terrified by the nearness of the fire, reared again. This time its rider was ungracefully pitched to the ground. As Magnus clambered to his feet, the stallion bolted towards the woods, riderless, and disappeared.

The rumpus of both the fleeing thief and the frenzied horse had alerted the two remaining aggressors, who noticed Magnus at the exact moment he noticed them. They were hardly a few yards away, hidden in the dark shadows of Helge's barn. Like their accomplices, their faces were covered. Grida was with them, her own face very visible – bruised and streaked with tears. The sight inflamed Jarl Erlend's son with anger. They had her gagged, which accounted for her recent silence, and one man brutally held her arms.

The other ruffian, surprised by Magnus's sudden appearance on the scene, instantly drew his sword.

The one holding Grida didn't even bother.

Everyone froze.

Magnus knew the dagger in his own hand was a joke. Against the two of them, both well-armed, a lone defender with a knife didn't pose much of a threat. But he wasn't going to back down. He had at least one weapon they might not want to mess with. He was the Jarl's son.

"Let her go," he demanded.

Oh yes, they recognized him alright.

The thug who had drawn his sword wavered, and cast an uncertain glance at his comrade. He half-lowered his blade, not sure what to do. The Jarl's son, after all!

But it was the other man, the one holding Grida, that Magnus realized he'd have to reckon with. This one seemed totally nonchalant, unconcerned that he'd been caught in crime by Erlend's boy, a prince. Through the cut-out slits in his mask, he boldly locked eyes with Magnus.

He, obviously, would not back down either.

Grida watched them, the gag choking her. She looked ready to faint with fright. Behind the four of them the fire kept raging. Its heat was tremendous.

"I said," Magnus repeated, "let her go. Now."

The eyes behind that mask flickered with amusement. Whoever he was, he had no regard for Magnus's princely rank. The reaction was disconcerting. Nor did he bother to draw his weapon. All he replied was, "Make me. I dare you."

Grida was pale as death. The second man glanced irresolutely from Magnus to his partner-in-crime. Then he lowered his sword and stepped back out of the way, indicating clearly that he wanted no further part of this. Wise man, Magnus thought. At least *he* knows the power of the Jarls.

"My father will have you executed for this," Magnus said to the bold one. "You will never get away with it. Release her this instant. I order you."

To his amazement the man started to . . . laugh.

It wasn't often that Magnus got angry, but now he felt his blood boil. It was not the personal insult to himself, nor even to his father the Jarl, but the bruises and terror on Grida's face and the fact that Helge's homestead was being destroyed before their very eyes. And to top it all off, this was his brother's sweetheart. Enough was enough. Magnus lunged at the man.

Well, that took him by surprise. He had no choice but to release Grida as his hands flew up to protect himself. In a flash Magnus threw him to the ground and tumbled on top.

"Run, Grida! Run!"

She certainly didn't need encouragement. Sobbing and half-hysterical, the poor thing fled.

The cowardly one made no move to stop her. In fact, he bolted in the opposite direction and fled too. *He* wasn't going to mess with Erlend's son.

The fight was easier than Magnus expected. His opponent,

taken unawares, had been too cocky to draw his weapon earlier, and now he was fumbling for his sword in vain. A few good smashes to that masked face and Magnus quickly had him pinned down.

Kneeling on the man's chest, he held his dagger to the marauder's throat. The other groaned in pain.

"I could kill you this minute," Magnus said. "Nothing would be easier. But I won't. My father and my uncle, Jarl Erlend and Jarl Paal, will have that honor. You'll be hanged for this."

The man was silent. He wriggled a bit beneath Magnus's weight, but his eyes, incredibly, remained fearless. "Oh, I really don't think so, Magnus," he said, his voice holding something akin to amusement.

The conceited and over-familiar words bewildered the Jarl's son. Who would *dare* speak to him like that. . .and at knife point?

Magnus released the pressure of his dagger against the man's throat and angrily ripped off his mask.

The smirking face looking back at him was none other than that of a fellow prince, his own cousin Hakon. He was Jarl Paal's only son and therefore the heir, jointly with Aerling, to the Orkney Throne.

Chapter Three

Jarl Paal was fed up. Fed up with decisions, fed up with problems, fed up with the heated disputes he and his brother Jarl Erlend perpetually had. And above all, fed up with his scoundrel of a son Hakon.

He breathed a sigh and rubbed his throbbing temples, wishing this crashing headache would just go away. He knew that, despite their muted conversations, all the Chieftains in the great smoke-filled Hall were watching him. He and Erlend together, as the two of them sat side by side upon their huge twin carved thrones.

He stole a covert glance at his brother beside him and felt a prick of annoyance. Erlend was chatting with his old friend Holbodi, laughing and sipping his mead-horn as if he hadn't a care in the world. To be sure, he could sit there, cool and calm as you like; after all, what had Erlend to worry about? The Chieftains would undoubtedly believe Magnus's story, not Hakon's. They always did. It wasn't fair, Paal thought, this continual pitting of brother against brother, cousin against cousin. Hakon was always at odds with Erlend's two boys. Today it was Magnus. Usually it was the older one Aerling. But it was inevitably one of them.

Our father should not have done this to us on his deathbed, Paal mused bitterly. Putting Erlend and me together on the same throne, Jarls with equal power. Who ever heard of two kings for the same kingdom? No wonder there were so many problems.

These last twenty-six years had been rough, yet at least *they* were brothers; what troubles would arise when their own eldest sons, Hakon and Aerling, eventually inherited their crowns? Paal greatly feared the kingdom of the Orkneys was in for major turmoil.

Next to him, Erlend refilled his drinking horn, still rapt in jovial conversation with Holbodi. The man was a landowner originally from the Hebrides, and he and Erlend were the closest of friends. Their cheerfulness irked Paal; how could they be talking about ordinary things like crops and repairing the fishing boats at a time like this, when Erlend's very own nephew, one of the kingdom's heirs, was about to stand such serious trial? It seemed inconsiderate, to say the least, and Paal blew up.

"I can't believe," he snapped at Erlend, "that you are going to do this to me. Bringing my son to trial before the Council like this!"

Taken aback by the sudden outburst, Erlend lowered his drink and turned to look at Paal. So did Holbodi.

"It's an insult," Paal continued, "and totally unjust. Hakon is innocent of this alleged crime!"

Erlend shot a glance towards the door, as if to say, *Where is your son Hakon anyway? He should be here by now,* but all he said aloud was, "I am sorry, Paal, that you feel that way. But we rule these Isles together, and if we want justice to reign, criminals must be punished. *All* criminals, no matter from what bloodlines. I can't help it if that includes your wayward son Hakon."

Paal felt the stab of his words, which, alas, were only too true. Hakon was a troublemaker and had been so from his mother's womb. But what could a father do?

"He may be unruly at times," Paal said, "but he is still my heir and one of the two future Jarls."

"That does not put him above the law, brother."

Holbodi gently cleared his throat. "My Lord Paal," he ventured, "your son Hakon committed a most grievous crime in burning down a Chieftain's farmstead the other day. Surely you understand that."

"Had not my own son Magnus," Erlend put in, "stumbled onto the scene and rescued Helge's daughter, I daresay Hakon would be up for another and much more debasing crime. You know it yourself, Paal."

Paal felt cornered. "You only say that, Erlend, because *your* heir has been interested in the girl for the last five minutes. If it had been any other lass on the island, you could not have cared less."

His brother flared. "*That* is an outright lie." Then he added, "And the only reason *your* heir chose *her* was to enrage *my* heir. Everyone in this room knows it."

Paal flinched. Of course it was true. In attacking Grida, Hakon had thrown a direct challenge at his cousin Aerling. It was so glaringly obvious.

To Paal's surprise, Erlend's voice suddenly softened. "I am a just ruler, Paal," he said, "and so are you. Our prime obligation should be to ensure law and order in this, our kingdom." His eyes were full of compassion. "If Hakon was anyone's boy but yours, you know he would be executed for what he did to Helge's farm."

Paal, searching for an excuse, said, "Hakon has his own side of the story." Indeed, Paal had heard it over and over again. So had the Assembly of Chieftains in the days preceding today's trial. "My son swears to me, Erlend, that Grida herself started the fire when she was cooking. He arrived there just in time to drag her out of the inferno. He saved her life."

Erlend cocked an eyebrow. "In a bandit's mask?"

"You have only Magnus's word for that."

"And Grida's."

"She could be lying too. Anything to pass on the blame. Do you think she wants to admit to her father that her carelessness destroyed his home?"

"Paal, don't be so naive."

Holbodi spoke up. "You are forgetting, my Lord Paal, about the three other offenders. Grida didn't just make them up."

"How do you know? No one has been identified. There are no witnesses that these other three mysterious villains even exist! Magnus and Grida could easily have fabricated the whole dramatic episode."

Erlend simply turned away. He was disgusted.

Jarl Paal fell silent. There was no point, he knew, in arguing his son's innocence further. Even he himself hardly believed Hakon's story. Incidents similar to this had happened in the past. Although none of them had ended in such devastation, Hakon had tried on other occasions to seize property that was not his by right. Usually his misdemeanors were done in the open, and often even in the name of his father the Jarl. He had gotten Paal into some very uncomfortable positions. But this time his masked face, his destruction of a valuable farm, and the attempted abduction of a Chieftain's innocent daughter were just going too far.

Suddenly Paal felt old, and very, very tired. In any case, it would not be he, nor Erlend, who judged his heir this day. Normally, yes, the two Jarls would decide the case and mete the punishment. But in this circumstance, the Chieftains had the final say. As soon as Hakon arrived, their verdict would be public, and Paal would have no choice but to submit to their decision.

He knew, deep down, that they would find Hakon guilty. It was just too obvious. His tale changed with every retelling, whereas Magnus's and Grida's versions remained the same. And the evidence --- the huge torches used to light the fire, the few valuables belonging to Helge found dumped hastily outside, the chaotic hoof prints of several horses --- all these things Hakon simply could not explain away.

Paal also knew that, yes, his son's life would indeed be spared. The Assembly could not execute one of the kingdom's two heirs. No one, after all, had actually been killed. But what Paal did not know was what punishment the Chieftains would impose. A fine perhaps, to be paid to Helge. Or they might make Hakon rebuild the house with his own sweat and toil. Whatever it was, Paal consoled himself, it could not be all that bad. After all, this lad was one of the next Jarls.

Just then, the Chieftains' spokesman, a respected middle-aged warrior by the name of Tor, approached the dais. He stopped before the twin thrones and bowed. "My Lord Paal, my Lord Erlend." Deference and respect were in his voice, yes. But something else too. Reluctance? Regret? Paal wasn't sure. He felt his heart sink.

"Where," Tor asked quietly, "is Hakon? He was meant to present himself over half an hour ago. The Assembly grows impatient."

Paal said, "I instructed him to come."

"Then I fear he is very late, my Lord Jarl."

Paal glared at him. "I said, my son will be here soon."

"Indeed," Erlend cut in with a frown, "so will Yuletide. Paal, send someone to fetch him. We have all had enough. Find him."

Paal redirected his frigid stare at his brother. "I notice your two sons aren't exactly punctual either, are they?"

"Aerling and Magnus are not the ones standing trial."

Before Paal could reply, the heavy doors at the far end of the Hall were abruptly thrown open. The entire gathering of men turned to look.

But it was not Hakon who entered. It was Aerling. He stormed in, his face flushed with barely concealed rage, his eyes instantly roaming the room for the cousin he no doubt wanted to slay.

"He better not have brought a weapon," Paal said quickly to Erlend. "It is expressly against the rules of this Council." Every man in this room, the two Jarls themselves included, were at this moment completely unarmed.

"My son knows to obey. He will have no sword, Paal. I guarantee it. Look for yourself."

Erlend was right. Paal could see no weapon. Aerling was unarmed.

"Thank God," Holbodi breathed, "there will be no bloodshed today."

Erlend smiled wryly. "I would not say that, my friend. The day is yet young." He, of all people, knew his eldest son.

Aerling reached the two thrones. "Where's Hakon?" he demanded without preamble. "Too gutless to show his ugly face, I'll warrant!"

"Aerling, that is not the way to greet your uncle."

But obviously the prince was not in a polite mood. "I'll kill him, Father! I swear I'll tear that beast limb from limb for what he did to Grida!"

Jarl Erlend's words came swift and sharp. "Speak not like that before the Council, son. You'll end with a dagger in your back."

"But Grida is *mine*! How dare he lay even a filthy finger on---" He stopped beneath his father's withering stare. Erlend always had control over his boys. *Always.* Paal would give anything to have some over Hakon.

They are so much alike, Paal thought. Aerling and Hakon. Both violent, both unruly hotheads. Two volcanoes just waiting to erupt. How would the kingdom possibly survive with those two insolent youths together on the throne?

Our father should not have done this on his deathbed.

The spokesman Tor said, "My lords, here comes Prince Magnus."

So quietly had the second son of Erlend entered that no one had even noticed. He calmly came forward and stopped beside his older brother. The two gave each other a long and meaningful look, worth more than a thousand words, and Paal had the distinct impression his nephews had earlier been arguing and were continuing to do so now with their eyes. Nor did it require much imagination to hear their silent conversation.

He'll be dead meat when he gets here, Aerling's eyes were saying. *You just watch.*

Don't you dare, Magnus was silently replying. *You know it's a mortal sin.*

As if I care!

You had better care, big brother. Else you'll end up in Hell.

Despite himself, Paal was almost amused. Anyone watching could have easily guessed what was passing between them. After all, the whole kingdom well knew these two brothers.

But if their unvoiced quarrel was so very obvious, it was also obvious that Magnus had the upper hand. Aerling looked exasperated, which might mean, Paal hoped wildly, that Magnus would win. The younger one could do that; amazingly, he could actually quell the fury of his brother's temper. He was the only one on the planet who could.

Belatedly, and somewhat distractedly, Magnus tore his eyes away from their silent argument and turned to the two Jarls. "Father," he greeted respectfully. "Uncle Paal."

Jarl Erlend cleared his throat. "I'm glad you're here, Magnus. We're just waiting now for your cousin Hakon."

"He's on his way," Magnus told them. "I just saw him across the courtyard."

For some reason the mere statement was enough to re-inflame his brother. "Then you've seen him alive for the last time," Aerling fumed, "because in a few minutes, he's a corpse."

Magnus shot him a look. "Stop it, Aerling. You gave me your word you would leave him be."

"That was last night. I've changed my mind."

"You can't," Magnus told him simply. "You're too honorable for that." He even smiled when he said it.

Watching the two of them, it was obvious to everyone that Aerling was fighting hard to control his temper. Maybe, Paal prayed in his heart, Holbodi would be proven right and there would be no bloodshed this day.

At that moment, however, the doors once again crashed violently open and Hakon finally swanked in.

"Here he comes," Aerling seethed. "Looks like he decided to ooze out from under his rock after all."

And that's when Jarl Paal spotted his son's poorly concealed sword.

Chapter Four

As if in a daze, Grida wandered silent and alone through the still-smoldering ashes of what had been, only days ago, her and her widowed father's homestead. The devastation was unbelievable; she could hardly take it in. Their cottage had been humble, and little within had been valuable in terms of wealth, but to Grida it had been a palace, and the memories it held were more priceless than gold. Now it was gone. Everything, destroyed. The sense of loss was numbing.

The acrid smell of smoke still lingered in the air around her as she stepped carefully over the rubble, stooping every now and then to pick up and examine some burnt and disfigured object. Her dress and hands were smeared with soot, and her eyes swollen from tears, but she was loathe to leave until she had found the box, the one her long-dead mother had left her.

She knew she should not be out here alone. If her father found out, he would be angry. And so would her Lord Aerling. All the warriors were this hour at the Council in the Great Hall, and no one was near to defend her if any of the other three attackers, still unidentified, happened to come back. Grida was afraid. But this should not take long, not if she hurried.

Nervously, her eyes darted back and forth to the surrounding woods, which now held an eeriness they never had before. The fearful memory of her attack was still so vivid. The knowledge that three of them had gotten away was disturbing enough, but what really terrified her was the identity of the one offender who had been unmasked. He had turned out to be none less than Lord Hakon himself, son of Jarl Paal and co-heir, equally with her Lord Aerling, to the entire kingdom. Nothing could have frightened Grida more.

The mere thought of him made her shudder. She had always been scared of Prince Hakon, even as a little child. He was creepy. She remembered how she would run to the other side of the road, or hide behind her father, whenever she had found herself in his presence. Now she was more scared of him than ever. Especially because she had had to testify against him --- the prince himself!--- in front of all the Chieftains. The Assembly had questioned her, over and over again, about every terrible detail of her attack, and although the accused had not been present, surely he would know everything she had said. What might he do to her now? Her only consolation was that her rescuer was himself a prince; surely the Chieftains would believe Lord Magnus's story, even if they were inclined to doubt hers. Between the two sons of Erlend, Grida could not have had more powerful protectors.

Despite this, her gaze continued to roam the lonely wilderness around her. After all, her Lord Aerling and his brother were not around and three of the masked bandits had escaped. They could be anyone . . . and *anywhere*. Truly she must hurry and find what she was after.

Finally Grida glimpsed it, a charred corner of the trunk buried in the ruins. She stumbled over and knelt down on the ash-strewn ground, and worked the burnt box free. With the greatest of care, she fumbled to unfasten the latch and realized her hands were starting to shake. This was the thing she had returned for, but now that she had found it, she dreaded to look inside. How ruined would its precious contents be? She was just about to push open the lid when she heard a noise.

Grida jerked her gaze to the woods and she froze. A horse-backed figure was riding across the clearing, obviously straight towards her. She leaped to her feet, sudden panic rising. Should she run? Was it . . . one of *them*? In her fright she was rooted to the spot.

And then she let out her breath as she recognized the cloaked rider. It was only the noble Lady Thora, wife of Jarl Erlend and the mother of both her good lords Aerling and Magnus.

Within a few seconds her Mistress drew rein beside her and gracefully dismounted. No words were needed. Lady Thora understood everything. She simply pulled Grida against her heart in a motherly embrace and held her tight. Then she released her and said, "You should not be here alone, my Grida." It was a rebuke, yes, but a gentle one.

"I know, my Lady. Please do not tell Lord Aerling. He will be so angry with me."

"And so he should be. But do not worry; if he learns of it, it will not be from me." The Jarl's wife gave a wry smile and added, "My son is already murderous enough today. I have no intention of adding to his wrath, I assure you."

"Is the trial over?" Grida asked. "What happened to Lord Hakon?" Just saying his name made her feel almost sick and Grida had to fight down the temptation to hatred rising up inside of her.

"I know nothing more than you do," Lady Thora said, "except that the Assembly is taking an unusually long time. But, Grida, come away. You must not be here."

Grida's gaze dropped to the box at her feet, still unopened. She hadn't had time to take out its contents, although in her heart she knew that what lay within, like everything else, was probably ruined forever. She felt the threatening tears start to sting her eyes and reached up to wipe them away.

Lady Thora saw, and she followed Grida's gaze to the burnt trunk. Then, to Grida's astonishment, the Jarl's wife actually knelt down in the grime and the ashes, jeweled cloak and all, and opened the chest herself. She gently lifted the once pristine white garment, now blackened beyond recognition, handling it as if it were a treasure. Which, to Grida, it was. Then Lady Thora looked at her questioningly.

"It was," Grida sadly explained, "my mother's wedding dress. My father had saved it for me."

Compassion filled her Mistress's eyes, but there was nothing Lady Thora could say to console her. Ever so delicately she refolded the spoiled bridal gown and placed it back in the chest. "My poor Grida. I am so very sorry."

Grida blinked back the tears. She had never truly believed she would someday wear it as Prince Aerling's bride. How many others before her had also wildly hoped to be chosen by the handsome heir, only to be disappointed in their young love? It would take an awful lot, after all, to domesticate someone like him and make him want to settle down; he was a warrior through and through. But dreams were free and Grida had indulged in them, as did every nobly-born maiden in the kingdom.

But seeing the once exquisite bridal gown now lying in ruins seemed somehow symbolic to Helge's daughter and shattered her hopes.

Not reading her thoughts, Lady Thora said softly, "I remember the day your mother wore it. She looked so beautiful. She really did. I cannot tell you, Grida, how sorry I am for everything that has happened. I am so ashamed of my nephew Hakon."

"I am tempted, my Lady, to despise him for this."

The words just tumbled out before Grida could stop them.

Hatred was a terrible sin . . . she was horrified it could even have entered her mind.

But once again, Jarl Erlend's wife seemed to understand. "It is only natural for Satan to tempt you to hate Hakon. Do you think the devil would let such a perfect opportunity for temptation pass?"

"I . . . I guess not, my Lady. Not when you put it that way."

"But do not worry, Grida. Feeling a temptation is not the same as giving in to it. You must expect these feelings against Prince Hakon; they are normal after the terrible things he did to you and your father."

"Yes, my Lady."

"My nephew committed a most atrocious crime. But the Council, I promise you, will punish him for it." Suddenly her Mistress's tone took on an edge of anxiety and she added, "If, that is, my son Aerling does not kill him beforehand."

Grida had not thought of that possibility. She knew her Lord Aerling was obviously enraged by his cousin's attack on her, but to think that he might take vengeance into his own hands had never even entered the girl's mind. The idea was horrifying. "But my Lord Aerling must forgive too," she said innocently. "I have. And so has my father."

"Have you, my dear Grida?"

"Oh yes, my Lady. Our Father in Heaven commands us to. How can I not?" To Grida, there were no other options. She did not *feel* forgiveness in her sentiments, but that did not matter. It came from the will, not from the emotions. Every Catholic knew that.

"God must be very pleased with you, Grida, for pardoning such a terrible offense. You will be blessed for it, I am sure." Then Lady Thora sighed and confided, "I doubt my son Aerling can forgive as readily as you and your good father have. Pray for him, Grida. Forgiveness is difficult for all of us, at times even heroic,

26

but between this kingdom's two heirs, it will require, I'm afraid, nothing short of a miracle."

Grida saw Lady Thora's gaze travel in the direction of the faraway Assembly Hall and there could be no mistaking the profound worry in her eyes.

Whatever was taking so long in the Great Hall, Jarl Erlend's wife obviously feared the worst.

Chapter Five

Making a show of bravado, Hakon swaggered from the wide flung open doors towards the royal dais. To everyone else in the crowded Hall he no doubt looked smug, as if he had not a worry in the world, but Jarl Paal could see the fear which lurked beneath his son's apparent nonchalance. It was something perhaps only a parent could pick, but Hakon was scared, and with very good reason. It was the surest proof of his guilt, and to Paal nothing could be more incriminating . . . unless, that is, anyone apart from himself had seen the hilt of his son's poorly hidden sword.

Of all people, it would have to be Aerling. Naturally.

"Hey!" Paal heard him demand. "What's that under his cloak?"

It was glaringly obvious what it was. The Chieftains' spokesman Tor quickly turned to Paal. "It is forbidden, my Lord Jarl, to bring a weapon into the Assembly."

Paal already knew that and felt like a fool. Had not he himself, mere minutes ago, shot the same rebuke at Erlend when Aerling had stormed in? Yet Aerling had not been armed. Hakon was. Paal thought, *Of all the stupid young puppies. Couldn't he ever do anything right?*

"Well, well," Hakon smirked, arriving before the twin thrones. "Look who's here. It's Magnus, the holier-than-thou-liar. Fancy that. Deary me."

Magnus made no reply. Aerling looked murderous. Jarl Paal quickly said, "Son, put down your sword. Immediately. It's against all regulations."

Hakon ignored him. He was too busy giving Magnus that hate-filled cute little smile which said, *My word against yours, cousin.*

Paal tried again. "Hakon, I said give up your sword. Now."

Hakon heaved an exaggerated sigh and rolled his eyes, as if his father's authority was something to be borne with a martyr's patience. Every Chieftain in the room, all of whom were themselves unarmed, was watching to see if their Jarl could control his renegade son. As the terrible seconds ticked by, Paal was sickeningly sure that Hakon would disregard his command completely.

Then finally, feigning boredom, Hakon deigned to unbelt the concealed weapon and flung it to the floor. It landed with a clatter beneath one of the two thrones. Paal found himself emitting a breath of huge relief.

What a boy to raise. Then again, maybe he only had himself to blame.

Jarl Erlend was the one who broke the awkward silence. "It is late," he said. "Let us proceed."

Hakon shrugged. "Proceed all you want. I am protected by the law."

"Not," Erlend said tersely, "if found guilty, young nephew." He went straight to the point. "Three days ago a prominent nobleman and member of this Assembly lost his home in flames. His daughter was captured, threatened, and could have been killed. Or worse. These charges are not light and you, Hakon, stand accused. What have you to say in your defense?"

Hakon looked his uncle defiantly in the eye. "Grida started the fire when she was cooking. The strumpet is not only careless, but the world's biggest two-faced liar."

That did it. The volcano that was Aerling erupted.

Hakon had no time to dodge. One second they were two normal people standing beside each other, as normal people do; the following second they were a violent rolling heap on the floor. The Hall was instantly filled with the excited din that any good brawl will elicit amongst warriors. The fight was all the more rousing being between the kingdom's two heirs. Paal realized to his horror that none of the Chieftains had any intention whatsoever of intervening; they were content to leave Hakon to fend for himself. In fact, they were cheering Aerling on.

Magnus was the only one in the room to react. He plunged straight into the fight, but only in an attempt to rip Aerling off their cousin. "Stop. You're going to kill him."

"You bet I am," Aerling shouted back, thrusting his brother out of the way. He must have thrown him a lot rougher than he had intended, for Paal saw Magnus badly winded and he stumbled to the side, unable to breathe.

It was all happening too fast. Aerling had Hakon on the floor now and was on top of him, locking his cousin in a brutal grip by the throat. "Get him off me!" Hakon squealed. They were the last words he could get out before Aerling began to strangle him. Paal started to rise, alarmed, from his throne. His son's face was rapidly turning a sick shade of purple, his tongue beginning to hang out. Paal saw Hakon's right arm sweeping wildly across the floor as he groped in desperation for the sword he had moments ago discarded, but it was well beyond his reach. Aerling's hands were like steel claws, and a strange gurgling noise was rising from Hakon's throat. Paal was suddenly frozen; his legs refused to cooperate anymore. His son was being throttled to death right before the entire Council. Would no one intercede?

As if in answer to his unspoken prayer, he saw his youngest nephew fly at them a second time. Magnus had recovered from his brother's unintentional blow and once again went straight for the fight. All three were on the floor now, Magnus trying to pry Aerling's vice-like grip from around their cousin's throat. But he couldn't. Aerling was too strong.

"Let him go," Magnus was shouting. "Aerling, let go." But his brother was way beyond reason and would never release his prey now. It was a build-up of a lifetime of enmity, all the hatred the two heirs had for each other had finally spilled uncontrollably over. Hakon should never have touched Grida; there was no way Aerling was going to have mercy on him this time.

Then Paal saw Magnus do the unthinkable, something no one but a madman would do. It was an absolute last resort, the only way left to save Hakon's life. Magnus brutally grabbed his brother's collar, jerked his face towards him, and actually punched him. Once . . . twice . . . and both times *hard.*

Paal couldn't believe his eyes. He thought, *You young idiot. You're dead too. Get out of his way, nephew, FAST!*

And it looked like Magnus had indeed done the last heroic thing of his life. He shot to his feet faster than lightning, and Aerling, blinded by rage and pain, released Hakon and flew after him. Paal knew the younger boy didn't stand a chance. There was no getting away, no point even trying to run. Magnus spun around and faced his brother bravely. "You promised me," he shouted. "You swore you would not kill him in cold blood."

Unbelievably, those few simple words made the exploding volcano pause in its eruption.

"You swore it, Aerling." Magnus had less than half a second to plead his cause. "Leave Hakon to the Council. Don't lay his murder on your soul."

For a heart-stopping moment the two sons of Erlend faced each other like a pair of wild young bulls. The room fell deathly quiet; no one in the Hall was cheering now. Nothing could be heard but the three combatants' ragged breathing and Hakon whimpering like a whipped puppy on the floor. But no one was looking at Hakon anymore. The bruises on Aerling's face were swelling rapidly and looked spectacular, one straight over the eye. His brother must have smashed him unbelievably hard.

Paal realized that he, along with everyone else, was holding his breath. Jarl Erlend had long ago sprung to his feet, but for the first time in his life, even he had no hope of controlling his boys right now. Of one accord, several Chieftains urgently started to move forward to save the younger prince. But they needn't have bothered, because at that moment, to the amazement of all, Aerling relaxed.

"Alright, Magnus," he muttered. "Not for anyone else but you."

It was over. A hundred warriors let out their breath.

Looking relieved beyond anything, Erlend's youngest son calmed down too. Paal saw that Magnus was badly shaken, and not one man here could blame him for that. Hardly a dozen warriors in the kingdom would dare have taken his brother on. Aerling, although only in his early twenties, was a formidable match for anyone, let alone a seventeen-year-old boy. He reached up and gingerly touched the places where Magnus had punched him; Paal had no doubt those welts must hurt like the blazes. Nonetheless, Magnus moved now to stand beside him before the two thrones, trusting that his brother would not hurt him. No one could believe what they had seen.

The sound of groaning on the floor suddenly drew everyone's attention back to Hakon, who had been temporarily forgotten.

Erlend's friend Holbodi had quietly gone over and was now reaching down to offer him a hand up. Hakon's breath was coming in huge gulping gasps, his color a ghastly hue. His shirt was soaked through with perspiration; his hair plastered with sweat. A stream of blood was trickling from his nose, dripping onto his clothes. He looked simply atrocious. But at least he was still alive.

Barely.

Paal thought, *That was close.*

Holbodi was standing there, trying to help him, but Hakon was too dazed to notice. In the shameful silence, he clambered to his knees, only to lurch forward and fall again to the floor. It took another two clumsy attempts before he finally managed, with Holbodi's help, to stand upright. Once there, he swayed on his feet and regarded Aerling with a look of open fear. Nowhere to be seen was his former bravado. He wiped his bleeding nose across his sleeve and angrily jerked away from Holbodi's supporting arm. Then he stumbled over beside Magnus, putting the younger boy as a barrier between himself and Aerling, for obvious reasons. He seemed to have no idea that his younger cousin had just saved his life, even at risk of his own. If he did realize, there was certainly no trace of gratitude in the way he looked at Magnus. His eyes held nothing but hatred for both of Erlend's sons.

The room was embarrassingly quiet now, except for those pitiful gulping noises still coming sporadically from Hakon. Jarl Paal had never been more mortified in his life. It was all the more humiliating in that Aerling wasn't hurt in the least, apart from those ghastly bruises inflicted by his own courageous brother. He wasn't even breathing hard! Paal felt his cheeks grow hot with shame for his stupid offspring. Feeling an absolute idiot, suddenly wanting to kill his son himself, he stepped back to his throne with what little dignity he could muster and sat back down. He was sweating nearly as much as Hakon was.

Considering the appalling shape his own son was in, Paal was shocked to notice the way in which Aerling was looking at the one who had stopped him. Despite those terrible bruises on his face, or rather because of them, Aerling was regarding Magnus with an almost amused newly-found respect, as if to say, *Not bad, little brother. Never knew you could hit so hard. I'm impressed.* No one else seemed to notice, least of all Magnus.

Jarl Erlend was angry now and was unable to hide it. "Let's proceed with this trial," he ordered. "Tor, you're the spokesman for the nobles. What have you to say?"

Tor cleared his throat, obviously embarrassed for the sake of Jarl Paal. Although in theory he addressed both Jarls, he kept his eyes locked on Erlend. "My lords. The full Assembly of Chieftains and I have examined the evidence and compared all three stories, not only once but multiple times. We reached our unanimous verdict early this morning."

Hakon, incredibly, had regained a remnant of his former nerve. "You can't punish me!" he spat out. "I happen to be the next Orkney Jarl." But when he said it, he made awfully sure he was out of Aerling's range.

Tor looked uncomfortable, but was unyielding. "To the contrary, Hakon Paalson," he announced calmly, "the incident at Helge Stianson's farmstead was the last in a rather long line of transgressions and insurrections. Were you of baser blood, you would without question be executed for this crime. As it is, your life shall be spared." He cast a look at Aerling and couldn't help adding, "By the Council, at least." Even Tor, who in his younger days was without doubt one of the best fighters the Orkneys had ever bred, was unable to hide the admiration in his eyes.

Hakon would not dare bring himself to glance at his two

cousins. But to the spokesman he gave a smug victorious smile. *See*, it seemed to say, *I am above the law. You just proved it.*

But the smirk was not to remain long upon that insolent face as Tor delivered the unexpected blow.

"Your life shall indeed be spared," he repeated, "but your claim to the Orkney throne has by this crime been forfeited. You are no longer an heir to the crown. Your cousin Lord Aerling shall inherit all."

Jarl Paal was shocked. Speechless. So were his brother, his son, both nephews. None of the royal family had expected this. Aerling was too stunned to even look triumphant. Paal didn't know who was more dazed, his own son or Erlend's. He thought, *No! This sentence is too harsh. They can't do this to my boy!*

But Tor and the Chieftains obviously did not think the punishment unfair. "Furthermore," the spokesman continued, his voice the only sound in the dumbfounded silence, "you shall be exiled forever from this kingdom. As of now, young Hakon, you have one day with which to depart these Isles. Twenty-four hours. Exactly. Not one minute more."

Hakon reeled, as if he had been physically struck. His wide eyes darted from Tor to his father and back again. "You – you can't do this to me!" he blundered, his voice estranged and frantic. "Father, stop them! This – this is an outrage!"

Outrage or not, harsh sentence or fair, both Jarls' hands were tied. For once, their power was overridden.

Paal could not think of anything further to say. "Hakon," he managed, "I am so sorry."

"You're *sorry?*"

"Son, I --- "

"You can't let them do this! Father, you are the Jarl! It's within your power to stop them!" Hakon's eyes were wild with fear and bewilderment.

It was Jarl Erlend who answered him. His voice, although firm, held a genuine note of compassion. "I am afraid, nephew, the Assembly has ruled. Your father is helpless, as am I. It is you, sadly, who have outlawed yourself. No one else in this room, Hakon. Simply you alone."

At those words, Hakon savagely looked away. His gaze rested on Magnus standing beside him and his eyes burned with rage. "It was *YOU!*" he yelled. "*You* outlawed me, Magnus!"

Jarl Paal felt his heart contort. The intensity of hatred in his son's eyes! It frightened even him!

"Hakon," he pleaded, "my son, I implore you. Take your punishment like a man. Can you at least do me that honor? For once?"

He could not believe he had just said that, and out loud! Here he was, a king, and his tone was reduced to that of a beggar to his own child. Every warrior in the room heard it. What could be more humbling for a Jarl?

The look on Hakon's face distorted itself into something almost inhuman. He spoke again, but this time his words were very low and meant for no one to hear except Magnus alone.

But Paal heard.

"This is your doing, Magnus. You hear me? *Your* doing! And I swear to you, by the gods, I will have your blood!"

He meant it. Oh yes, Hakon meant it!

Never had his father heard him speak so true.

Chapter Six

The boat was readying to sail. A small vessel, equipped for not more than a couple of men, but a sturdy craft nonetheless. From Magnus's position on the lonely clifftop above the sea, the boat looked to him like a child's model bobbing on the foamy water. But he recognized the sail. Oh yes, that he recognized.

It had been just over twenty-three hours.

The thin sound of Hakon's voice was carrying on the wind, yet at this distance the words were indiscernible. Someone was down there with him, but it was impossible to tell who. The wind was picking up and dark clouds were gathering in the sky. Magnus knew how quickly a squall could move in; their voyage would be an anxious one. He blessed himself and said a prayer for his cousin's safe passage. After all, he didn't want Hakon to actually die. Not with sin on his soul and vengeance burning in his heart.

Forgive him, please, Lord, Magnus asked. *He hasn't always been this bad.*

In fact, a strange sadness tugged at Magnus's heart and he pulled his cloak tighter about him against the raw wind. It had been many years since he and Hakon had gotten along. Far too many. But there had once been days, innocent days, when as little boys they had romped the wilderness together and carved their wooden weapons and staged the most serious mock battles. How many times they had slain each other in play --- frightful torturous deaths wielded by little blunt axes, skulls pretended to be smashed in --- then they had gone into peals of laughter at how much fun it had all been and immediately re-enacted the gory demise again. Oh, they'd had arguments too, without doubt. Plenty of them. Times when Magnus wouldn't play his part right and the older boy's eyes would turn to icy steel, and Erlend's small son would scramble away in stark terror, feeling sure that his cousin would kill him in reality. More often than not, little Magnus would fly straight to the protection of big brother, until he eventually learned how costly Aerling made Hakon pay, and vice versa. The fights of the big boys were never pretend, never merciful, and Magnus would usually end up crying in a lonely chapel somewhere, promising God in his childish heart that he would never run to Aerling again and be the cause of such sins. He understood somehow that poor Jesus was the One Who really got hurt, and slowly he steeled himself to bear Hakon's bullying alone and in silence. Thus they'd spent their childhood years in a kind of truce, sometimes playmates, sometimes not. But they had never been enemies. After all, Hakon was his cousin. They were blood.

That was the tie that held him, however estranged, to Uncle Paal's son. Simply blood.

With Aerling and Hakon, however, it was exactly the opposite. It was precisely that union of consanguinity, never able to be dissolved, which galled them both. Two heirs to the same throne, perfectly equal. Neither came first, neither was last. Oh yes, the same kingly blood pulsed through their veins and they hated each other for it. Hakon was slightly older, which Aerling as a child resented bitterly, but he managed to get his own back by being the stronger of the two, a fact which Hakon could never forgive . . . and which Aerling certainly never let him forget. Magnus, along with everyone else in the kingdom, had always dreaded the day when they would reign together as equal Jarls. Their vicious jealousy would have ripped the Orkneys to shreds.

But that would not happen now. Hakon was on a boat down there, disinherited and exiled forever, and the bizarre deathbed wish of their grandfather, Thorfinn the Mighty, had at last been made void. Aerling would inherit all.

Magnus noticed the storm was swiftly moving closer. He usually loved this isolated bluff with its rugged beauty and the grandeur of the ocean far below, but today it was foreboding and it chilled him. No matter how hard he tried, he simply could not stop thinking of his cousin's parting words to him.

I swear to you, by the gods, I will have your blood!

Blood. The very tie that bound him most closely to Hakon.

He strained his eyes to see the tiny figures below battling the rising wind and the flapping sail. Who, he kept wondering, was that second man on the boat? He must be one of Grida's other attackers.

"It's that rat Ofeig. That figures, doesn't it?"

The voice at his shoulder came out of nowhere. Magnus's heart all but leapt out of his chest. Wildly he spun around.

Instant relief washed over him. "Aerling, you startled me. I didn't know you were here."

"I can see that."

The bruises on his face looked awful. Magnus felt bad. He wondered if he had actually cracked a few bones or something. He had intended to hit his brother hard, but not quite as hard as *that*.

On the other hand, maybe love-struck little Grida would think they made her Prince Charming even more handsome. Girls were funny creatures, Magnus was discovering. Especially girls in love. Things like unsightly black eyes actually impressed them. Grida would naturally assume that Hakon was the villain who had punched her dashing hero, which was far more romantic than him being hit by baby brother. Let her believe it. Magnus wasn't going to tell.

He turned back towards the sea and said, "You shouldn't sneak up on people."

"And *you* shouldn't be standing out here unarmed and not even paying attention. I did it on purpose, you little idiot. Don't you realize I could have rammed my sword straight through your spine just now and you would have been dead before you even realized anyone was behind you?"

Aerling was right, of course. Magnus had been caught off-guard and if it had been someone else, he might be splattered all over the beach right now. But he simply said, "Hakon has about forty minutes left."

"Thirty. I'm timing it, believe me. But don't go changing the subject."

Magnus thought, *Here we go. Lecture time.*

"There were four men who razed Helge's farm. How many are on that boat, Magnus? Go ahead and tell me."

Magnus didn't answer. It was perfectly obvious how many there were.

"Go on. Tell me. You know how to count."

Magnus sighed. "Two."

"Right. Only two. Hakon and, like I just told you, Ofeig."

That's who the second man obviously was. Aerling would know. Ofeig was Hakon's cousin on his mother's side. No relation whatsoever to Erlend's boys.

"Which means," Aerling continued, "that there are two more somewhere else. You should've unmasked all of them. I hate to say it, Magnus, but that was incredibly stupid of you."

"Hey, it was four against one! What did you expect me to do, ask them for their autographs? For heaven's sake, Aerling, I didn't even have a sword!"

"And I notice you don't have one now either, do you? Good grief, Magnus. Standing on the edge of a precipice, alone and defenseless. Not the most intelligent thing in the world, is it? Look, I know this is a radical thought for someone like you, but guess what? You have enemies."

"I realize that. I don't need you to tell me."

"And you're not even sure who they *are?*"

"Alright, Aerling, you've made your point."

"Then you had better wake up awfully fast, little brother, or you're going to find yourself dead."

"I said, you've made your point."

"I certainly hope so."

The wind was picking up; a few drops of icy rain started to spatter the rocks around them. They watched the boat in silence for a few minutes. Then Aerling said, "I bet you anything it was the Sock brothers. Grida thinks so too."

Magnus looked at him. "You mean Sihvat and Gurd? I'd been wondering that myself. They've been slinking around a lot lately."

"So you've noticed too?"

"How could I not? Those two make my skin crawl."

Aerling hesitated, then went ahead and told him. "Apparently they had a nasty dispute with Helge a few weeks ago. Grida said they threatened her father; they even had *him* quite scared. I seriously hope for your sake that it wasn't them."

Magnus thought, *So do I.*

Everyone knew the Sock brothers were devils. Both Jarls had been trying to nail them for years. Problem was, no one could ever catch them red-handed.

"If only you hadn't let them get away," Aerling said. "Father could have finally hung them."

Despite himself, Magnus was getting fed up. "Look," he said, "I did my best. I was just a little preoccupied, in case you hadn't heard, trying to save your precious little lady's life. Would you rather I had gone after the others? Go ahead and tell me."

His brother let up. "You're right," he said, softening. "I apologize. I don't even want to *think* what Hakon might have done to Grida if you hadn't been there. You were very brave and, well, I'm proud of you."

The words were unexpected. Coming from Aerling, that was the compliment of a lifetime!

"Forget it," Magnus replied. "I only did what anyone would do." And he thought to himself, *Give me four armed bandits any day. It took a lot more courage twenty-four hours ago taking you on, believe me.* But he wouldn't dream of admitting that out loud. What he did say was, "If it was Sihvat and Gurd, I guess I'll just have to live with it, won't I?"

"Good luck. Those two are exactly the type to stab you in the back and dump you over a cliff-face. Just like I could have done easily five minutes ago. I'm only going to tell you this once, Magnus, because I know you're not stupid. But you watch those two. I mean it. No more traipsing around the island without at least a knife. At *least!* Understand me?"

"Yes."

"Good. About time. And keep one hidden under your blankets too."

"Just to change the subject . . . you're sure it's Ofeig on the boat?"

"Oh yes, it's Ofeig alright. I knew you'd be wondering so I came to tell you. I'm surprised you can't recognize him, even from way up here. No one else in the kingdom comes anywhere close to being that ugly."

That made Magnus laugh. There was certainly some truth in that statement. And, thinking about it, it made perfect sense. Ofeig would have been the one who had drawn his sword at Helge's barn, then had wavered and run away, unwilling to mess with Magnus. He was strangely loyal to his cousin, but also greatly feared the power of the Jarls, being related to Hakon only on the maternal side.

"He'll be leaving, I guess, to avoid execution, in case I ever try to identify him."

"Exactly," Aerling agreed. "The man may be ugly, but at least he has a brain floating around somewhere between his ears."

"Speaking of floating," Magnus said, "there goes the boat now."

Sure enough, the ropes were untied and off she set through the churning waters. The freezing rain began coming down harder.

"Do you think they'll make it through?" Magnus asked, "That swell is beginning to rise."

"Frankly, I hope they both die. But even if they live, at least Hakon is gone forever. I'm so happy I could sing a Te Deum."

"Pity you don't know the words," Magnus said sarcastically. "Maybe you should learn them, along with a few other basic prayers. Namely, the Our Father." He gave his brother a loaded look and added, "I'm sure you can figure out which phrase I'm talking about. I'll even give you a little hint. It has something to do with trespassing."

Aerling didn't deign to reply.

After a moment of rather chilly silence, Magnus decided it to let it drop. Preaching would accomplish nothing. He had learned that over the years. Only God's grace could change his brother's heart and Magnus prayed for it daily. He wouldn't stop either, until God gave in.

"Where do you think they'll go?" he asked.

"Who cares? Valhalla, the moon, it's all the same to me. Hakon can drop off the edge of the world and no one springs to mind who would miss him." Aerling laughed. "Maybe his mother. Even that's questionable."

Hakon was Jarl Paal's only son. No brothers to grieve his shameful departure, nor to pounce on his half of the forfeited throne. Paal had four daughters, but they couldn't claim it either. Aerling had it made.

"Lucky for you," Magnus dared to say, "that I stopped you from killing him yesterday. Because if you had, you would be the one on that boat." He couldn't resist adding, "And I don't have to tell you . . . do I? . . . who would be the next Orkney Jarl." Not that Magnus wanted it! It was the absolute last thing he desired in life. Give him a humble monk's cell, or, if God so willed, a devout wife and a family. But to rule a kingdom? No thank you. Magnus wouldn't want that responsibility for all the world.

Under the circumstances, therefore, he was surprised to hear Aerling mutter under his breath, "I was so close yesterday. *So close.* I almost wish you had let me do it. Not one other person in that Hall was going to stop me."

Magnus knew it was true and the knowledge was disturbing. A whole room packed with Catholic warriors, and hardly one man had not been cheering Aerling on to murder. Magnus just could not understand how, after over a thousand years of Christianity, the meek and gentle message of the Crucified had penetrated so few hearts in this cold Viking world. Didn't men know there was no manliness in sin? No nobility in violence? Even poor Aerling, for all his excellent qualities --- and he certainly had many --- did not understand much.

"All I needed was a couple more seconds and I would have had Hakon burning in Hell."

Magnus turned on him sharply. "And you would have ended up there too, right beneath him. Just think about *that*. You and Hakon together . . . *Forever*."

Chapter Seven

(Sweden, two years later)

The night was moonless. As the two horses faltered their way through the gloomy woods, the rider at the rear felt vaguely uneasy.

"Hakon," he said, "this is crazy. Let's turn back."

"Not on your life, Ofeig. What do you think --- does this look like the right place to you?"

"How should I know? All these Swedish hovels look the same to me. Especially in the dark."

Hakon pulled rein and glared at his cousin. "Well you're the one who took directions from the old beggar in the last hamlet. Did you pay attention, or didn't you?"

Ofeig bristled. "Look, all he said was to ride five miles north and we would hit some run-down shack where this fortune-telling hag is supposed to live. Whether directly north, or northwest, or northeast, he didn't say. If you don't trust me, then why didn't you ask him yourself?"

Hakon gave him a smoldering look and moved his horse on. Ofeig reluctantly followed. The dead leaves crunched beneath the animals' hooves much louder it seemed in the dark than they should have. Somewhere a lone owl hooted. The sound mournful, almost foreboding.

"We're lost," Ofeig said. "Just be humble and admit it."

"No we're not. Look. Over there."

"Where?"

Hakon pointed. "Right in front of you, blockhead. That building in those trees. See it?" Once again he halted his horse.

Ofeig leaned forward in his saddle and strained his eyes. Sure enough, a lopsided shack could be glimpsed between the bare swaying branches not far ahead. "You call that a building? More like a chicken coop, if you ask me."

"Whatever. I bet this is the place."

"Certainly. I could see a witch living there. Suits the character."

No sooner were his words out than a strange orange glow suddenly appeared from one of the windows.

"See?" Hakon said. "What'd I tell you? She's expecting us, even now. She just lit a lantern to guide our way."

Ofeig didn't normally believe in this sort of stuff, but for some reason he felt his skin begin to prickle. Maybe it was just the power of suggestion; he wasn't sure. "Are you certain you want to do this, Hakon?"

"I wouldn't pass it up for the world. She's supposed to be the best fortune-teller in all Scandinavia. They say she can see anyone's future."

"For the price she's going to charge you, cousin, I'd claim the same ability too." Ofeig let out a laugh. "I've got it! Maybe that's the business you ought to get into --- Hakon the Mighty Soothsayer. I bet you'd end up richer than you would have done as the Jarl of Orkney."

"Shut up, Ofeig. That's not funny."

"Come on, Hakon. I think this whole idea is childish. No one can see the future." Then he grinned and added, "Actually, I take that back. I can." He closed his eyes and swayed in his saddle, feigning a trance. Then he said in a made-up spooky voice, "I see clearly, Hakon Paalson, that in ten minutes from now, you will have lost what few gold coins you have left." He reopened his eyes and asked, "How's that for a startling prediction? And I don't even have a crystal ball or anything."

Hakon glared at him. "You're just scared, that's all. A coward. What are you afraid of? The devil's power?"

If this woman's power truly was from the Evil One, then yes, Ofeig might be scared. But he knew it wouldn't be. "The crone will be a fake," he said. "Take my word for it. Witches don't exist."

"Really, Ofeig? Then why are you so eager to turn back?"

It was a challenge and Ofeig knew it. All he replied was, "You're insane. I always suspected as much, but now I finally know."

"You know what? You are really starting to annoy me."

"Alright, alright. This is your little adventure, not mine. I wouldn't be caught dead consulting a sorceress."

"Fine. Then wait outside." Hakon slid off his mount's back and thrust his reins at his comrade. "At least hold these."

"With pleasure."

Hakon narrowed his eyes and asked, "Uh, what was her name again?"

"Hiedawaart."

"Hiedawaart? Are you sure?"

"That's what the beggar told me. Hiedawaart the Wise." Ofeig couldn't hide his amused smile as he said it.

Without another word, Hakon headed off through the trees. Ofeig watched with a mingling of curiosity, doubt, and not a little humor as his cousin swaggered towards the rundown hut. Did he imagine it, or did their two horses grow skittish?

Before Hakon could knock, Ofeig heard the door creak open and a dark shriveled figure appeared against the flickering orange glow.

Hmm, maybe she *was* expecting them.

"What do you want? It's past midnight." Even her voice fit the part. It actually cackled! Ofeig bent closer to watch and listen through the screen of trees.

"Are you . . . um . . ." Hakon wavered.

Ofeig grinned. So, who was scared now?

"I'm looking, uh, for a woman named Hiedawaart the Wise." To Ofeig's great satisfaction, his cousin sounded unnerved. "Is that, uh, you?"

The old hag chortled. Kind of like a chicken. "People have called me by that name, yes."

Somewhere nearby a wolf howled in the night. Hakon nearly jumped out of his skin. Ofeig's grin only broadened and he decided that maybe this was worth coming for after all.

Long gone was Hakon's swagger, and his voice came out just a little too shaky as he announced, "Forgive me for the late hour. I come from afar. I'm, um, interested in my future . . ."

* * * * * *

When Hakon emerged from the black shadows of Hiedawaart's lair forty minutes later, his cousin could see he was visibly shaken. In fact, he stumbled towards the horses, white as a ghost.

"Give me my reins, Ofeig!" he blurted. "We have to get away from here! Now! Quick!"

"You look terrified, man. What happened?"

Hakon was just about reeling. He leaped onto his horse and yelled, "Later! Let's just get out of here!"

"Why? What did she do? Dump you in her stew and try to eat you?"

Hakon was clearly in no mood for his jabs. He whirled his

49

mount around, booted it savagely in the flanks, and disappeared through the tangle of dead trees at breakneck speed.

For some reason, his fear proved contagious. Ofeig whipped his own mount and pursued him recklessly through the sinister woods.

* * * * * *

"Slow down!" Ofeig begged. "We're riding too fast. You'll get us both killed."

The witch's den was a good couple miles behind them and it was a miracle they were both still alive after such a blind charge in the dark. A hundred branches had reached out to snare them; a dozen times their steeds had nearly tripped; both men and beasts were scratched and sweating.

"Stop," Ofeig called out again. "Take it easy, Hakon."

His cousin slackened the pace to a brisk trot, then his horse slowed to a staggering walk, and finally came to a standstill. Ofeig pulled up, gasping, beside him.

"Just relax, will you?"

"I'm trying, alright?"

"Old gorgeous is miles back there. Get a hold of yourself, Hakon, and tell me what happened."

Hakon was breathing hard, but his initial terror at least seemed to be subsiding. "She was pure evil, Ofeig! Honestly, that's the only word to describe her. She was possessed, or . . . or something. I'm still sweating."

"Well, cous, don't say I didn't warn you."

Hakon took a deep breath, starting to calm down.

Ofeig waited patiently. This was going to be good.

"First thing she does," Hakon began, a quiver in his voice, "she rips out a fistful of my hair. I mean, she just grabbed hold of ---"

"You can't tell me that frail old relic actually clawed out a chunk of your hair and got away with it."

"Listen, do you want to hear this or not?"

"Believe me, I'm all ears. But knowing you, old Hiedawaart should be dead by now. So why isn't she? Admit it, Hakon. She robbed you."

"Alright, I admit it. Somehow, and I honestly don't know how, she confiscated my weapons as soon as she let me through the door. It's like she just took them and I didn't even know how. Then she cleaned out all my money. But listen, I don't even care. I ---"

"You don't even *care?*"

"No, it's not important."

"Well, she must have *really* cast a spell over you!"

"Of course she didn't! But, Ofeig, the things she prophesied!"

"Prophesied my foot. You're so gullible. But go ahead. She magically makes your money and weapons disappear, tears out a handful of your precious hair, and lives to tell the tale. Good. Then what?"

Hakon's expression was dead serious. "She gets some little bones. They were human, I swear it! She mixes them with my hair and makes this potion with other stuff and ---"

A yelp of laughter escaped poor Ofeig. "You mean she made a soup with your hair? Sounds great! I love it!" He narrowed his eyes and solemnly asked, "Question is, can we eat it on a Friday?"

Hakon glared at him. "Stop it, Ofeig, or you will be the dead one." He was getting angry. "This is serious, can't you tell?"

Ofeig cleared his throat. "Excuse me. Of course it is."

Hakon continued his tale. "The witch goes into a kind of trance. You should have seen her! It was creepy. She's swaying and chanting and her eyes go all funny. I was ready to bolt, I can tell You. Then she begins to speak. Only it wasn't her voice anymore.

It was . . ." Hakon shivered and dropped his voice to an awed whisper, ". . . it was . . . the Devil."

That was too much. Just too much. Ofeig exploded. He fumbled in his saddlebag for something with which to wipe his eyes.

Hakon watched him with fire. "Laugh all you want, you oaf. But it's true. And do you want to know what else is true? The things she revealed about my future. They *will* happen! You just wait."

Well, Ofeig couldn't say he wasn't intrigued. True or not, he was dying to hear what the seer had said. He quickly composed himself, lest Hakon refuse to tell him after all. "Go on," he said, straight-faced. "What is this your marvelous future?"

"There's two things."

Suddenly Hakon hesitated, as if, coming this far, he no longer wanted Ofeig to know.

"Well?" Ofeig prodded.

He could tell Hakon was torn. Shame flickered across his face, for an instant only, but Ofeig had seen it. There was dishonor somewhere in that prophecy and Hakon wanted to hide it.

Now Ofeig *really* wanted to hear. He sobered up instantly.

"Go on. I won't laugh this time. I promise."

Hakon sucked in his breath. He would not look his cousin in the eye. "She told me," he said quietly, "that in a few years' time I will commit a heinous sin, something so inhuman I will hardly be able to atone for it. Ever."

So much build-up, for *that*? Ofeig was deeply disappointed. "You call that a prophecy? Everyone sins. Who cares? You've already fulfilled it anyhow. Plenty of times. Don't tell me you've never noticed?"

"That's not what she meant, Ofeig." Hakon's fleeting moment of shame had already passed. He looked his cousin squarely in the eye and said, "Besides, that's only the first part. The second half is much, much more interesting."

"I certainly hope so, for everything she took."

Unexpectedly, Hakon smiled. It was a smug, triumphant smile. All his earlier fear had vanished. He looked suddenly like a victor after the war.

"She told me . . . Are you ready for this, Ofeig? She told me my life will be a source of stirring events and that someday I will become the sole ruler of the Orkneys, and my sons after me. Do you hear that? The *sole ruler.*"

"You mean, you alone will be the Jarl? She actually said that?"

"Could I be making this up?"

Ofeig frowned. How could this hag have known she was speaking to the outlawed prince of a kingdom? "Did you tell her who you are? You must have. Be honest, Hakon."

"I revealed nothing of my identity. I swear it, Ofeig. She just *knew.*"

Ofeig wasn't laughing anymore. In fact, he felt those little prickly bumps again. "You've been exiled, Hakon," he said quietly. "Your inheritance is gone. Poof. Vanished. Doesn't exist anymore. It's Aerling's now. All of it."

They looked long and hard at each other. Those facts were true. Hakon was at a loss. So was Ofeig.

Finally Hakon spoke. "Well, I'll obviously get it back. Don't ask me how or by what means, but that throne will be *mine*, not Aerling's. And I think I have just decided where to start."

"Really? Where?"

Hakon grinned. "Back to Norway," he announced.

Ofeig's heart sank. "You have to be joking. We've just spent the last year in Norway. All that place has to offer is a lot of moose and snow. No thank you."

"You're forgetting about our kinsmen there."

The two of them were cousins on the side of their mothers, both of who were descended from the royal Norwegian line.

"Uh, precisely which kinsmen are you meaning?"

Hakon's grin broadened. "The king, of course. None other. He has warships, and manpower. Plenty to spare. He'll help me. Wait and see."

Ofeig was unimpressed. King Berrfott had been reigning hardly a year. He was only twenty-three years old, even younger than they both were. Everyone knew he had little experience with war.

"Why should he help you? He may be distantly related to us, but he has never met either one of us in his life."

Hakon was unperturbed. "You'll see," he repeated, growing excited. "I'll convince him, and I think I know how." He threw Ofeig a grin and said, "In Norway, my good cousin, begins the fulfillment of my destiny."

Chapter Eight

The young King Berrfott of Norway studied Jarl Paal's son here before him with annoyance. He could not believe the audacity of this kinsman of his, who had simply strutted into his court, uninvited and unannounced, as if he owned half the palace just because his mother was remotely related to Berrfott's own. As if that wasn't bold enough, Hakon had actually demanded, right then and there, a fleet of warships and more than a few of Berrfott's Viking warriors to man them. Just who did this deposed Orkney princeling think himself to be? The Roman Emperor?

"What you are requesting of me," the king said, "is not slight. Armies do not grow on trees, Hakon Paalson. At least not up here."

"I realize it sounds like a lot, your Majesty, but listen to me. Victory is a foregone conclusion. I will reclaim my crown, with or without your help. It is my destiny, written in the stars. You will regret it, I assure you, if you send me away."

Berrfott tried not to laugh. Written in the stars, was it? Hah! What an idiot this Paalson fellow must be. Ignoring the ludicrous claim, which wasn't worth wasting breath over, he simply said, "Let me make sure I have understood this correctly. You actually expect me to invest my time, my gold, and my men --- at great risk to my own country, mind you --- in an attempt to help you, a complete stranger, overthrow your paternal uncle, Jarl Erlend, and his heir, whom you happen to dislike. Am I right?"

"You are perfectly right, your Majesty."

The insolence of this man was fascinating. Berrfott had never seen anything like it.

"All nice and cozy from your point of view, Paalson," he said. "But why should *I* be so eager to entangle myself in your personal vengeance?" Granted, they were related somehow way back in their bloodlines. Apparently Berrfott was equally kith and kin with that unsightly gargoyle waiting for Hakon in the hallway. But what were blood-ties? That was nowhere near being an adequate reason to stake his own regency on what might easily turn out to be a disaster.

"You mean," Hakon asked, "what's in it for you? Is that what you're concerned about?"

The king couldn't help but smile. Of course that was what he was concerned about. "Seeing you have phrased it so bluntly," he said, "then yes. That is exactly what I mean."

"There is more in it for you than you can dream of."

"Convince me. May the luck of the gods aid your tongue boldly."

Now it was Hakon who smiled. A conceited, know-it-all smile which Berrfott did not like. He stepped closer to the throne and purred, "Just think, your Majesty, what jewels lie beyond the Orkneys. The Hebrides, Ireland, England. They are all there for your taking, except for the unfortunate fact that *my* kingdom has always stood in Norway's path." He paused, letting that sink in. "But we can easily fix that. You and I together."

Berrfott considered. So that was the bait. Ireland. England. Oh yes, beautiful jewels, both. Despite himself, the young king could not help but be dazzled at the thought. He, and his father before him, and his grandfather even before that, had long coveted those lands. And yes, as much as he hated to admit it, a few useless strips of dirt like the Orkneys, for all their smallness, had always lain there stubbornly in the way.

Hakon continued. "If you help me get my throne back, I promise to grant your fleet safe passage through the seas. Everything west of the Orkneys can be yours. I will even aid you." He winked conspiratorially. "We can do together what no army has accomplished in decades. You'll go down in history as one of the great Norse heroes, more famous than even Harald-Halfdanarson. Think of the legends that will spring up around you. Or, rather, around us. Because you can't get around the Orkneys, your Majesty, without my help."

Berrfott could not deny the truth of that, nor the attractiveness of the proposal. He was definitely interested. But, still, it was risky.

"What makes you so certain, Paalson," he asked, "that an attack on your Isles will not end in ruin for my own kingdom of Norway? After all, your father and uncle are very powerful warlords themselves. All Scandinavia knows this. The Orkney Jarls are not to be trifled with."

"You seem to forget, your Majesty, that every military hides a weakness. Several weaknesses, in fact. You have yours, my father and uncle have theirs . . ." He smiled and spread his hands, the picture of innocence, as he let the sentence hang temptingly.

Berrfott leaned forward eagerly in his throne. "And the weaknesses of your islands you are willing to divulge? What are you? A patriot or a traitor?"

Hakon laughed. "A patriot, of course, my good king. My cousin Aerling and his younger brother had me exiled by an evil conspiracy. They had been trying to outlaw me for years. In wanting to overthrow them, I have only the welfare of my people at heart. This Aerling would be a tyrant on the throne. The kingdom trembles even now with fear at the thought of his reign."

But the king of Norway was hardly listening anymore. His mind was racing, his heart beating fast with excitement. Maybe this could work. Maybe it actually could! England, after all, and Ireland! Forget about Hakon and his rival cousin: Erlend's two sons were small stuff. There were much more urgent things to address.

"How will I get in?" he asked. This was the first problem. "Your father and uncle will spot my warships miles away."

Hakon wasn't concerned in the least. "Not," he said, "if there are no sentries to see the fleet. I know where they are posted, and where they are not. There is a way to sneak in, I assure you. No one will ever suspect."

"What are you talking about?"

They were alone in the room; nonetheless Hakon lowered his voice. "There is a shoreline on the remote side of the island, nicknamed by the locals Suicide Bay. There are no farms there, and no watchmen, because it is assumed, and quite rightly, that any invader would not survive its treacherous rocks. The bay is a deathtrap, but only a part of it. Those who know the place intimately, and the seasons of its tides, can navigate it safely. I could get a boat through there with my eyes closed."

Berrfott was listening intently. "But an entire fleet of warships?"

"Leave it to me, your Majesty. I know what I'm talking about. By the time we're spotted and the alarm raised, it will be too late. The battle, if there even is a battle, will be over before anyone knows what hit them. It will be the easiest conquest of our lives!"

Berrfott drew in his breath, his mind calculating. "Let us say, Paalson, that this plan of yours works. We slip in undetected and actually make it to the fortress. What about these relatives of yours?"

"Do whatever you want to my uncle Jarl Erlend. He's all yours." Hakon paused, and Berrfott could see sudden hatred sweep across his face. "But I want his heir dead. His heir, and also the younger brother. Those two. We slay them."

Berrfott cocked an eyebrow, intrigued by the unexpected vehemence in his visitor's voice.

"The heir, I already know, is Aerling. Who is his brother?"

"Magnus. Torture them both and torture them good. Then I get the honor of killing them."

Berrfott did not answer immediately. Paalson's ideas no longer matched his own. After all, the two sons of Erlend, if captured, would be worth an impressive ransom.

"I do not," he replied, "necessarily require their deaths."

"But I do! It's part of the deal!"

The king felt a sharp prick of annoyance. The so-called deal would be whatever he made it, not what Hakon wanted. They were his ships in question, and his warriors, every one of them. He would decide who lived and who died. Hakon's impudence bridled him, but he remained kingly calm.

"I shall want all the information you can give me. A map of this bay and anything else out there that might concern us --- nearby farms or shepherds' huts and the such like --- you know the type of thing. I don't want to stumble on any heroes who think they can raise the alarm. I will not mess with Jarl Paal and Jarl Erlend unless you eliminate all risks to my army. Do you understand?"

"You shall have everything you need."

"You do realize," Berrfott warned, "that should I let myself be persuaded by you to undertake this expedition, I will show no mercy to the countries I conquer. I will treat them alike. *All* alike. Do I make this clear?"

It was Hakon's turn to look annoyed. "The Orkneys," he said tersely, "are mine."

Just who did he think he was? No, the Orkneys would be Berrfott's, and his alone. Every square inch of them, every rock, every blade of grass. Hakon Paalson was an idiot. He was going to learn reality the hard way.

Let him. He was nothing but a pawn. Something to be used and discarded.

The king of Norway said, "You have a father there, and a mother, I presume. Who else? Any siblings?"

"Yes. Four sisters.Why?"

"I have already warned you that I will show no mercy." He let his eyes bore into his kinsman. "Just how badly, Paalson, do you want your throne back?"

A flicker of hesitation passed over the other's face. But if he was torn, it did not last for long. He answered firmly, "I want it very badly."

"Very?" Berrfott smiled, satisfied. "Then you shall have it," he lied. He stood up, the audience over.

Already he was starting to laugh inside. Oh yes, he would get the Orkneys alright . . . and keep them for himself. After that, all the isles in the great sea beyond.

What a fool of a son the great Jarl Paal had bred. If every man in the Orkneys possessed this little of brains, Norway's campaign west was going to be a Sunday picnic.

Chapter Nine

(Several months later)

The middle of a savage battle, Jarl Paal knew, was a strange time indeed to be suddenly missing his son. There were much more urgent and desperate things to be thinking about right now, mutilation and death not the least of them, and it annoyed him that at a moment like this the thought of Hakon should rise up out of nowhere to haunt his fatherly heart. But he couldn't help it. He simply missed his boy. It had been over two years now since Hakon's banishment. The possibility of dying, right here on this bloodied and trampled ground, never having another chance to see his son again, was heartrending.

Everywhere around him men were fighting for their lives --- in the courtyards, in the woods and open fields, in their cottages. The invading army had materialized out of nowhere, with no warning whatsoever. They had simply rushed out of the misty fields with their gleaming broadswords and spears and fearsome battle-axes, as if they had simply dropped from the sky, and began to butcher everyone and everything in sight. Nonetheless, Jarl Paal, and Erlend too, were impressed and proud of the brave response of their Orkney men. No one had run, no one had tried to surrender. Just the opposite. Everyone had rallied to the alarm, not only the Chieftains, but ragged peasants and farmers, and fearless youngsters too. Men and boys were out here in swarms, crude weapons clutched in hand, defending themselves and their kingdom against the enemy onslaught with a courage neither Jarl had ever seen before.

Paal himself was in the midst of it, fighting as he had not fought for many years, ever since he and Erlend had sided with Harald Sigurdson in the legendary battle of Stamford Bridge in England. But he had been young then and stronger and full of noble ideals. Now he was middle-aged and tired and it took all his strength to simply stay alive. Whoever the enemy was --- and he didn't even know yet --- they had come in hordes, hundreds of them. Paal greatly feared his own intrepid warriors did not stand a chance. The attack had been too sudden, too unexpected, to prepare any kind of organized defense.

As he swung his own huge sword back and forth, he knew that his brother Erlend was fighting likewise for his life, between moving among their Chieftains and giving commands, trying to create some degree of order in the confusion of battle. But surely Erlend must realize, as did Paal, that they were already as good as dead. They were vastly outnumbered, vastly unprepared, and there was nothing anyone could do about it.

His nephews were also out there, Aerling and Magnus, and Paal knew that both of them, like their father, could rouse the fighting blood of nearly anyone. The men would follow them, fight for them, die for them. Jarl Erlend's sons were loved by everyone.

The thought brought a fresh pang of sadness to Jarl Paal's heart. Where in the wide world was Hakon right now? He had been a rough one to raise, no question about it, but he certainly could fight and if he were here now he would do his father proud. Paal never doubted it for a moment.

But of course that would not happen. Hakon simply was not here. He knew nothing of this terrifying invasion.

Paal kept fighting. By nightfall, he feared, their kingdom would be shattered.

Chapter Ten

Magnus had never, in all his nineteen years, seen such ferocious fighting. Blood ran in pools upon the earth; it stuck to his sword, making its hilt slippery; it dripped down his shield and armor. The combat was a massacre, and he knew, as he swiped and slashed his way through the wild invaders, that the battle would not last long. There was simply no way the Orkney men could hold out. Not against these barbarians.

He had already been struck more than once but was still on his feet and that's all that mattered. He could feel a sticky wetness spreading across his shirt beneath his mail and knew it was blood, lots of it, but he ignored it and kept fighting. It would take an awful lot more than a few gashes to get a son of Erlend down. He wondered who the attackers were and why they had come, but what was most bewildering was how they had gotten in undetected in the first place. How had the sentries not spotted an entire army? It was unbelievable!

Well, it hardly mattered now. They were here and despite the fact that it would require a miracle to drive them back, Magnus wasn't going to give up. Nor would anyone else. The Orkneys had never bred cowards . . . except maybe one. But *he* wasn't here, and the rest of them would defend their homeland with all their might and main. Still, for every foe that fell beneath his own heavy sword, Magnus's heart beat a prayer for that man's soul. These were fellow human beings, after all, each one of them created and redeemed by the same loving God. The thought of mutilating and butchering as he was doing now was not Magnus's idea of fun, but he had no choice, so he fought with every ounce of strength and skill he had.

He lifted his wooden shield just in time as a massive piece of steel arched towards him, and managed to repel the blade's deadly blow. To his left someone was screaming in agony, at his feet a body thrashed on the ground. In the back of his mind he wondered fleetingly about his father, his brother, his Uncle Paal. Were they still alive? At least his mother, Lady Thora, was safe, and that afforded some consolation. As Providence had arranged it, she was far from harm's way with Magnus's two sisters, Gunnhild and Cecily, visiting relatives on another of the Orkney's small isles. They would be spared, and for that Magnus thanked God.

Another horned giant was rushing at him, an enormous bloodied battle-axe raised for the kill. Magnus leaped to the side to avoid the weapon's lethal thrust and was barely able to deflect it with his own sword.

And that's when something in the distance caught his eye.

He froze, unable to believe what he was seeing.

Impossible. It could not be. But . . . it was! In a flash, Magnus understood everything. How they had come . . . and why.

An unbelievable sense of pain ripped through his knee and he felt himself thrown by the impact. He found himself suddenly lying on the ground, hardly able to breathe. There was a rush of warm thick liquid pouring down his leg. He was not even sure where the axe had struck him, but all he knew was that he had to get out of its way and fast. Rolling onto his back, he thrust his shield above him in an almost hopeless attempt to protect himself from the deathblow that was about to follow. He could see the massive blade directly above him, coming down. Then there was a bone-shaking jolt and a terrible splintering crack as the timber of his shield was rent in two beneath the Viking's axe. For a moment its blade remained wedged in the wood, then the broken shield dropped to the ground and the axe was free. Magnus had nothing left with which to protect himself. Frantically he tried to scramble out of the way as his attacker once more lifted that giant weapon for its final chop. Magnus knew he was as good as dead. He tried to formulate some prayer, some act of contrition, but his mind was strangely paralyzed with fear. Murdered by an axe . . . what a way to go.

But amazingly no strike came. Out of nowhere a Chieftain flung himself at Magnus's assailant and with a mighty swing of Orkney steel a severed arm and axe both went flying through the air. There was a hair-raising scream and a contorting body thudded straight on top of Magnus. Blood was jetting everywhere. Then the grotesque burden rolled to the ground and the Chieftain rapidly finished him off with his sword. The rest of the fighting had already moved on. Struggling to catch his breath, Magnus attempted to wipe all the splattered blood off his face. He recognized Tor bending over him, helping him up.

"Tor," he gasped, "thank you." In his heart he thanked God too. He was actually still alive. Then he instantly remembered what he had seen, the thing that had distracted him in the first place. He must tell his father! He struggled to his feet, and nearly collapsed.

"My Lord Magnus, you're wounded!"

Strangely, after that initial strike, there was no more pain. Adrenalin was surging through him and, now that he was out of danger, there was only one thought on his mind. "My father. Where is he, Tor? I have to find him!" His mind was reeling at the memory of what he had spotted several moments ago in the distance. Jarl Erlend had to be informed!

"I have not seen him," Tor replied. "But your leg, my lord! Please, allow me ---"

"I'm fine! Tor, please! This is urgent. I must find my father." He pulled himself away from the Chieftain's supporting grip and looked frantically around.

"I don't know where he is, but I think your uncle is somewhere over ---"

"No," Magnus blurted. This was not for Jarl Paal to know! "Where is my brother then?"

Tor pointed helplessly in the direction of the fortress. "I glimpsed him that way a few minutes ago."

Magnus could see that the fighting in the shadows of the tall walls was just as desperate as everywhere else, but was visibly thinning out. And little wonder, if Aerling was over there. He could take on four at a time when he really had to.

"Alright," Magnus said, "I'll find my brother." Not giving Tor a chance to stop him, he headed straight back into the bloodbath.

* * * * * *

It was not easy for Magnus to make his way through the chaos of battle, but Aerling was in sight now, just a few yards away. A writhing figure was on the ground beneath him, clutching his head in those last terrible seconds as blood and brains pulsed out. He certainly would not be giving the Orkney heir any more trouble today. Aerling had already turned his attention to the next one, not even noticing the man's agony in his own desperate fight to stay alive. Magnus found the sight abhorrent, just as ghastly as what he himself had just been through, and he looked away, unwilling to watch such a horrid death. Another human being, after all . . . even if he was the enemy. But Magnus too had sent plenty of souls into eternity this day, all of whom had died in equally gruesome ways. It was kill or be killed, simple as that. All of this butchery, he knew, was the sin of someone else, the unjust invader, and before God the consciences of every Orkney warrior was clear in that regard. They were merely defending the kingdom which the good God had given them.

He waited until he saw a brief gap in the fighting and his brother was for a moment safe, then he called out, "Aerling! Over here." There were others to keep going . . . but Magnus must talk to him, urgently. "Aerling," he yelled again.

His brother turned and saw him. Magnus could hardly recognize his face, streaked as it was with sweat and spattered with blood, exactly as Magnus realized he himself must look to Aerling. But for all that, he appeared triumphant.

"Magnus," he called back, raising an arm as if in victory. "Can you believe it? We're actually holding them off."

Maybe *you* are, Magnus thought, but things aren't looking so bright and cheery anywhere else.

Without warning, weakness overcame him. It happened so fast he stumbled and nearly fell. Magnus should have known this would happen. Adrenalin alone had gotten him this far, but now delayed pain came flooding back through his leg with unbearable intensity.

Suddenly his brother realized Magnus was wounded, that the blood saturating him was actually his, and not only that of dead foes splattered on him in battle. In a flash Aerling was beside him, his look of triumph instantly gone. Magnus heard him spill a whole chain of foul oaths, then he said, "Let's get you to safety. You're about to pass out."

"Forget me. Aerling, listen. I have to tell you this! I just saw ---" Oh no, his brother was right. All of a sudden the world started to spin and everything was blacking out.

He was vaguely aware of being helped to the shelter of the fortress wall, and the clamor of battle faded into the background. He had the impression he was out for a minute or two, then there was water to drink and things were coming into focus again. The pain in his leg was unlike anything he had ever known. But there was something important he had to say---what was it? It came back.

"Aerling, we're in big trouble, even bigger than we thought. Even if we win this battle, we ---"

"Just shut up and hold still! I'm not listening right now." Aerling was kneeling on the ground beside him, examining the place where the axe had sliced him open, somewhere around or through his knee. He wasn't even sure himself where all that agony was centered. All he knew was that his brother was blazing mad. "What a mess! Great. How am I supposed to fix *this?*" Magnus knew neither of them had these precious moments to spare. The fighting was fierce and they both had to get back out there.

"Alright," Aerling muttered, "this'll work." He ripped a flask off his belt, which certainly did not hold water, jerked the top off, and started to pour the burning alcohol directly into the wound. Just like that, no warning whatsoever. The sensation of fire was unbelievable. Things were getting blurry again, awfully fast. Aerling must have realized, because he shoved the flask into Magnus's hand. Magnus didn't need urging. He drained its entire contents, grateful for every numbing drop.

In the meantime, after having so brutally disinfected the wound, Aerling hastily started unstrapping his own breastplate, then mailshirt, both of which he pulled off and dumped on the ground.

"What are you doing?" Magnus asked, shocked. "Why are you

taking your armor off?"

Aerling ripped off his outer shirt and began tearing it into strips. "In case you haven't noticed, you're bleeding to death. I need to bind this, fast." He looked Magnus in the eye and asked, "Ready for some fun? This is going to be tight."

Magnus thought, *there's my warning.* When Aerling used the seemingly innocent word *tight*, his idea was not that of your average person. Then again, neither was his strength. It was somewhere in the middle of all this torture that Magnus remembered why he had come over here in the first place. As soon as he could manage to speak at all, he gasped out, "I saw Hakon. He's . . . fighting on . . . the . . . other side."

Well, that did it. He certainly had his brother's full attention now.

Aerling froze.

"What did you just say?"

"Hakon. He's with them." His knee hurt so bad his eyes were stinging. It wasn't easy to talk. It wasn't easy to breathe! "And I think . . . Ofeig too. Not . . . sure."

Aerling was staring at him, stunned, as the implication of what he was saying sank in very quickly. Now he knew why they had been invaded. This was not just some random Viking raid. Hakon knew *everything,* every defense, every weakness, everything! His knowledge could bring the whole kingdom down, even apart from this one battle.

Aerling didn't say a word, not one single thing, and when that happened Magnus knew he was in the most lethal mood of all. And did it ever show in his eyes right now. Magnus thought, *I'm sure glad I'm not Hakon if my brother finds him.* He had been able to prevent Aerling from strangling their cousin two years ago, but if he got hands on him today, Hakon was dead meat on a block.

70

Finally Aerling spoke. "Keep still. I mean it! Let me finish this so I can get back out there."

"Go. I can finish it myself. Then I'll join you."

"Oh no you won't, little brother. You're done for the day, understand me?"

It wasn't wise to cross Aerling in a mood like this, but Magnus did it anyhow. "I said I'm coming too. What do you expect me to do, just sit here and read a good book while ---" Suddenly it hurt too much to continue. His brother had gone back to tying things up and speech was out of the question.

"I'll re-do it later with stitches," Aerling was promising further torture, "but at least now you won't bleed to death." Then he added, not very consolingly, "I hope." He threw a desperate look over towards the fighting, obviously dying to get back into it, then ordered, "Show me where else you're hurt. Hurry."

"Nowhere. I'm fine."

"Your mail's been slashed. Look at your shirt. I think you're bleeding beneath."

Magnus glanced down at his chainmail and realized his brother was right. The links had indeed been severed. No wonder he felt soaked underneath; he must be bleeding badly. But Aerling didn't have time for this. He, of all people, was needed urgently in battle.

Magnus hesitated, then insisted. "I'm fine, Aerling. Honestly. They're nothing but a few scratches."

His brother studied him indecisively for a moment, then gave in. "Alright. I'll try to send someone over to have a look. Maybe Grusp. He shouldn't be fighting anyhow. He's too old; he's going to get killed." Aerling jerked his mailshirt back over his head and stood up. He quickly started fastening on the rest of his armor. "Listen, I hate to leave you like this, but my time over here has really run out. You stay put and I'll come back as soon as I can."

"No. And don't bother sending Grusp because I'm coming with you. You can't stop me."

Aerling raised an eyebrow. "Oh really? Have you forgotten just whom your future king is?"

"You're not the Jarl yet, at least not that we know of, and I'm every bit as stubborn as you are."

Aerling said, "Fine. Go ahead and get up." He stepped back to watch. "By all means, lead the way."

It wasn't anywhere near as easy as Magnus thought it would be, but he managed to stagger half-way to his feet. Agony bolted through him, and it was only by grabbing onto the wall that he kept himself from falling. He realized there was no way on earth he would be charging around that battlefield anymore today.

Aerling just gave him one of those *I told you so* looks and watched him sit back down.

Then know-it-all big brother *finally* showed a little sympathy. He would not be happy being down either, so he said, "I'll make a deal with you. Hakon is *mine*, if I can find him. But Ofeig's head can go by your axe. I promise to save him, just for you."

Magnus knew the heir was offering him an honor. By law, the punishment for Ofeig's treachery would be execution, by that same fearsome weapon Magnus had so recently faced himself. But he only smiled and said, "Too easy. What's one swipe with an axe? I could behead him with my eyes closed. If I get Ofeig alive, I'd rather deal with him my own way."

Aerling looked impressed. Little could he have guessed what his brother was thinking. Magnus had in mind *real* weapons, like prayer and sacrifice. Ofeig had a soul; why couldn't he be converted the same as anyone else? That was a much more noble challenge than going at the fellow with an axe-blade.

72

"He's all yours," Aerling promised. "Do whatever you like. And I hope he survives this day, so you can get your hands on him."

"So do I. Believe me."

At that moment, their father's friend Holbodi came rushing over. "My Lord Aerling," he blurted. "Your father and uncle have both been captured! You must surrender the fortress immediately!"

It was over.

Their kingdom was gone.

Chapter Eleven

It had been a glorious day.

King Berrfott of Norway strolled alone through the corridors of his newly acquired fortress, high in spirits and well-filled with wine, as he mused how everything had gone so perfectly according to plan. His plan, that is, if not that of his incredibly conceited kinsman, that impudent Hakon Paalson. As if Berrfott had intended for a moment to actually give him the conquered Orkney throne. Not a hope in Hades. The kingdom of scattered isles might be small and relatively insignificant, but it was a kingdom nonetheless and it belonged now to Norway. Nothing like adding to the collection, Berrfott thought with a smile.

Outside the fortress walls an occasional disturbance could still be heard, although the fighting itself was over and had been for some hours. It was merely his men dealing with the messy aftermath that came with any conquest. There were dead to be buried or burned, bodies to sort through and wounded to be helped, and of course plenty of hostile and stiff-necked locals who needed to be brought to reason, by violence if necessary. True to his word, King Berrfott would show no mercy. What was the point?

But the most major issues, he had made sure, were already taken care of. Both Orkney Jarls, Paal and Erlend, were safely tucked away on the vessel which would bear them to their new home in Norway. A dungeon fit for a king. Or rather, two kings. They could rot there till the day they died.

As for the two sons of Erlend, the names of which Berrfott had temporarily forgotten, they were at this very moment being chained in a disused cargo-hold of another boat. The flagship, in fact. They, in a sense, were more valuable than their father, for they were worth a considerable ransom. Which was why the king had ordered them to be put on his own ship, even if it meant taking them half-way around Europe with the rest of his fleet. Overthrowing the Orkneys with such ease had emboldened him to continue his westward campaign as Hakon had suggested. The Hebrides were next, and the Sundry Islands. After that, who could tell? Maybe one day Ireland truly would be his. That would be the conquest of a lifetime.

He realized, however, that in regard to Erlend's sons, he was going to have to be careful. All accounts warned him that those two brothers could prove troublesome. Hence the chains. He would limit their food and water to an absolute minimum too. Keep them alive and breathing, but not much more. He must remember to tell that to the crew.

His biggest quandary, the thing he couldn't decide, was what to do with that strange kinsmen of his, Hakon Paalson. And for that matter, what about Ofeig? The man was unsightly, but he sure could fight. Actually, Paalson hadn't done badly either. Berrfott had initially been minded to simply kill them both. They were nothing but worthless traitors; no Orkney Chieftain would be willing to buy their release. But thinking about it, if they behaved themselves, he might be able to use them someday. Not now, of course. Too soon. But who was to say what the coming months would hold?

Hmm. Berrfott stroked the beard he was trying to grow and considered. He supposed there would be no harm in letting the pair live. Just throw them on to one of his lesser ships and forget about them. As the old saying went, out of sight, out of mind. It would be rather like fattening a couple of pigs for the slaughter. Yes, that's what he would do.

"Papa! Papa, is it really true?" The excited voice of his eight year old son Sigurd broke upon the king's thoughts as the little prince came scampering down the hall, followed by his warrior bodyguard. He stopped before his father and blurted, "Are you truly going to let me be king?"

Berrfott had to smile. It was Sigurd's first taste of war and what father could not be proud of the bloodied hatchet he still clutched tightly in his small fist, as if he would never put it down. He had, after all, killed an Orkney boy with it whom he had found hiding in a barn.

"Yes, Sigurd," Berrfott answered, giving the lad's bodyguard a wink. "This fortress is yours until my return from Ireland. Rule it carefully and listen well to the nobles who will stay to help you."

"You mean, everything is *mine*? Can I sit on the throne, Papa? Please!"

The king laughed. "You may sit there all you want. On either one of them. Remember, Sigurd, there are two." He bent down to be eye level with the beaming child and added solemnly, "You may even wear the crown. For mark well my words, my son: No descendant of Paal or Erlend shall ever reside in this fortress again. This kingdom belongs to Norway."

Chapter Twelve

(Four days later)

If there had been any way these iron manacles around his wrists could be broken by brute strength, Aerling would have done it by now. But it was impossible and he knew it. Like it or not, he and Magnus were stuck in this ship's filthy cargo-hold and there was nothing he could do about it. Not unless he could somehow come up with an object to pick the locks on their chains. Fat chance of that. He had been watching like a hawk every time their food was brought down, hoping against hope the Norwegian would accidentally drop something. No such luck yet.

He was determined to escape . . . hopefully with his brother, but if necessary alone. It was ridiculous to think that Magnus would be able to go anywhere, not in the shape he was in. But Magnus was not their father's heir. Aerling was, and his people needed him. He would return to them or die trying.

On the floor across from him, his brother was starting to stir once again from restless sleep. He was getting worse each day, and Aerling was awfully worried. Magnus had lost far too much blood and had received no further treatment for his wounds, apart from the little which Aerling himself had done so hastily on the battlefield. He had been simply appalled when the Norsemen had stripped his brother of his chainmail to put his shackles on, for it was only then Aerling had seen that Magnus's shirt was completely drenched with blood. Serious blood. Why hadn't the little idiot shown him those gashes when he could have done something about them? Nothing but a few scratches, he'd said. Right! Aerling was furious with him, but even more so with himself for not insisting to look. Well, too late now. He could not even get over there to try to do a single thing about it.

The length of their chains did not allow for much movement, a few feet at most. But they could lie down on the cold grimy floor if they chose to, which was better than not being able to stretch out at all. Their captors had even thoughtfully provided them with a couple of filthy blankets. Things that had not been near soap or clean water in decades. But it was freezing down here, especially at night, so they used them and were grateful.

Magnus managed to sit up and leaned back limply against the wall. He looked awful.

"How're you feeling?" Aerling asked. As if that question held intelligence.

"Just so tired," Magnus answered. "I don't understand it."

Aerling did, and tired wasn't the word. Magnus was exhausted from heavy blood loss, and obviously in terrible pain. Not surprising, considering those wounds. But little brother would never complain. No matter what. All he asked was, "Is there anything to drink yet?"

Aerling felt his blood boil. "No." It was infuriating. Since their capture they had been given very little food or water. Even Aerling was finding it hard, especially the burning thirst, and he hadn't even been wounded in battle. What must it be like for his poor brother? He shuddered to think. One thing he knew, it could quickly become Magnus's death-sentence to deprive him of sufficient water in his condition. How stupid could Berrfott be? It was so basic! If that odious little king wanted his big fat ransom for Magnus and himself, he had better start treating both of them a lot more humanely than this. The Orkney Chieftains were as loyal to their two princes as ever men could be, but they wouldn't pay out for corpses, Erlend's sons or not. What price was a pair of coffins?

Magnus, however, accepted his terrible thirst with no complaint. Aerling was amazed at how his brother appeared so resigned at taking all this. Almost peaceful, if he could use that word. It was as if suffering, now that it was here, was something Magnus valued.

As for himself, Aerling had spent the endless hours fantasizing about all the many and varied ways he could, given half a chance, kill the young king of Norway . . . and he had thought of quite a few interesting forms of death during these last days. He never knew he had such a gruesome imagination. But he *really* surpassed himself every time he thought of their traitorous cousin Hakon. For his death, Aerling had come up with a few ideas that even impressed himself.

"If only," he said under his breath, "he was chained up here next to me. I would make sure he had a voyage he would never forget."

Magnus knew exactly whom he was talking about. "Lucky for him and Ofeig they're not on this ship. But just forget them, Aerling. There's nothing you can do."

"Give me a knife and give over our cousin. That would be all I ever asked for again. I would disembowel him alive and force him to eat every greasy chunk of his own carved up --- "

"Stop it," Magnus said. "Your vengeance can't change anything. All it does is offend God, and He's been offended more than enough by what has happened so far. Do not add to it, Aerling. Please don't."

"I'm not the one," Aerling fumed, "who betrayed our

kingdom. Hakon is solely responsible for every dead Orkney warrior lying in our fields, and every widow and orphan left desolate today on our isles. Don't you dare preach to me about forgiveness this time, Magnus, because all I want is for Hakon to burn in Hell."

"Aerling, don't say that. For sure as God is God, you'll end up there yourself if you're not careful. What Hakon did is despicable and I'm not excusing it, but if we expect God to forgive us, we must first forgive our own enemies."

Aerling said, "Never." That was all there was to it.

Magnus really did look a wreck. Surely, Aerling thought, he was much too spent for an argument. But, no. Wrong. Stubborn little brother just wouldn't give up.

It obviously hurt even to speak, but Magnus said, "If you want to save your soul, you had better pray for the grace to be able to forgive our cousin. Because the way things are going, we might never see the inside of a confessional again in our lives. I mean both of us."

"Not even God Himself could expect me to forgive that Judas."

"Really, Aerling? Is that what you honestly believe?"

Aerling was feeling those first flickers of anger. It had been an atrocious few days and he wasn't in the mood for this.

Magnus said, "God can, and wants to, forgive all sins, no matter how terrible they are. Your sins, my sins, and, yes, even Hakon's. But He expects nothing less from us first. Nothing!"

"But it makes God seem so . . . so, I don't know what. Cruel or something!"

Magnus cringed at his words. "Oh sure," he said, "God is cruel alright. Cruel to the point of being crucified for each and every one of us. Is that your idea of cruel, Aerling? Dying for someone you love?"

"Stop it, Magnus. You're just confusing me."

"No, I'm not. It's Satan who's confusing you. He wants you in Hell. But I don't."

For someone as half dead as his little brother, he still had an awful lot of fight left in him. Aerling was amazed. Then again, maybe he shouldn't be.

Magnus continued, "Lucifer is the one tempting you to hatred, and he's been doing it for years and getting away with it. Please, Aerling, you can't let him keep winning."

"As if *you* know anything about temptation! You've never been tempted to sin even once in all your pious little nineteen years and don't pretend you have!"

To his surprise, Magnus actually flared. "Oh *REALLY?*"

He said it with such vehemence that Aerling instantly believed him. And thinking about it, yes, it had to be true. Aerling wasn't the only one that the Chieftains' daughters were forever chasing after, and even a devout lad like Magnus could not have failed to notice their continual vying to get his attention. He was only flesh and blood after all, and there were some suggestions Satan tried out on everyone, pious or not.

"Alright," Aerling said, backing off. "So you know about temptation too. But I bet you've never been tempted to hatred like I have. That's a totally different story."

His brief and uncharacteristic outburst past, Magnus returned to his usual self-control. "You're right," he admitted. "That's one thing the devil has never tried on me. Maybe someday he will, and I can only imagine it must be awful. I feel sorry for you." Aerling could tell he meant it. He could also tell that it was getting harder for his brother to keep up this conversation. He was really in pain; Aerling could see it in his eyes. "But Our Lord will give you the grace to forgive Hakon," Magnus continued, "if you ask Him for it. I shouldn't have to tell you all this, Aerling. You were educated by the monks of Eynhallow years before I was."

"Yes, and Hakon was right there with me. He turned out the pinnacle of holiness, didn't he?"

"Then pray for him. He needs it, badly."

Aerling couldn't believe his ears. There were limits after all! Surely his brother didn't expect him to actually fall on his knees and beg God to give that butcher a shiny halo and a harp in Heaven. He said, without really meaning it, "If God lets Hakon into Heaven, I think I'd prefer Hell for myself. At least then I would be rid of him forever."

Magnus winced, as if Aerling had physically punched him. "Would you just stop?" he begged. "You're hurting Our Lord with nearly every word you say and I refuse to listen to it."

"Fine, I'll stop. And *you* can stop examining my conscience for me. I am sick to death of a brother who thinks he's such a saint all the time. You want me to shut up? Then you can shut up first!"

Magnus did. Instantly.

As soon as the words were out, Aerling regretted them. His heroic little brother was already enduring more than enough suffering without him adding his own cruelty to it. Besides, he knew in his heart that Magnus was only trying to help him save his soul, and he should be grateful because he needed all the help he could get. But Magnus was *always* trying, and beyond a point Aerling couldn't handle it. Especially this whole forgiveness thing. If only salvation didn't hinge so heavily on pardoning one's enemies, then maybe holiness would be achievable, even for someone like him. There might even be a noble joy in serving the King of all kings. Magnus found it so. Why couldn't he?

Secretly, Aerling envied his brother. After all, how could one not admire the purity and inner strength that obviously came with loving God? Like now, for example. Magnus had made no reply to the brutal and unjust remark flung at him. He had merely taken it, humbly and with no trace of anger. That wasn't cowardice. It was the opposite. Utterly drained, Magnus closed his eyes. He was trying to hide it, but that knee of his must be killing him. Aerling wasn't stupid. He knew his brother was offering it up. Probably for him!

"I'm sorry," Aerling said, ashamed. "I didn't mean what I just said. That was cruel of me."

Magnus re-opened his eyes. "Forget it. It's been a rough few days. I don't blame you for losing your temper. You're the heir, not me. I can't imagine how it feels."

See how readily he could forgive? And even excuse! Just like the One on the Cross. Aerling felt awful. "Listen," he said, softening, "I will try, *honestly* try, to forgive King Berrfott of Norway. I mean that. All monarchs are greedy. It's normal. I'd probably become that way myself if ever I was crowned Jarl. So . . . well, I forgive him." He paused, then went further. "I will even pardon the puny Prince Sigurd. He's only a child and none of this is his fault. He can slobber all over my future throne as much as he wants, and I'll pray he goes higher in Heaven for it. Go ahead and think I'm lying, but I'm not."

Magnus was looking at him, amazed. But not nearly half as astonished as Aerling himself was. He couldn't believe he was actually saying this. Yet he was a man of his word and he meant it as best as he could.

Magnus said quietly, "Why would I think you're lying to me? You've never done that. Not once in our lives."

For some reason his brother's unshakable trust spurred him on to greater nobility, yet it was not without an interior struggle. This was getting hard. "I am even willing," he forced himself to say, "to forgive that despicable Ofeig. Now *that* borders on the heroic, believe you me, but I'll do it for you."

"No. For God. It has to be for God, or it means nothing."

Aerling knew he was right. He amended his words. "Then I forgive all three of them for God." He meant that too.

Magnus went awfully quiet. Was it was because he was shocked speechless, or because he was waiting for more? Aerling didn't know. Probably both. At any rate, he was saying nothing.

There was a silence.

Aerling likewise said nothing. The silence dragged. Became a little strained. Yes, Magnus was waiting. Of course he was.

But Aerling knew in his heart he could not go on. He could not promise his brother, or God, something fake, so he stopped right there.

Finally, softly, Magnus asked, "And Hakon? Do you forgive him too, Aerling? Please do."

For a long moment Aerling genuinely struggled with it. But it was useless. Too many hateful memories rose up in his mind. All his childhood fights with Hakon. Helge's home in ashes. Hakon's brutal attack on Grida, whom Aerling truly had loved despite the fact that he had put off marrying her for so long that she had finally disappeared behind a convent grille somewhere, radiantly joyful with her perfect Spouse, but leaving Aerling with his regrets. Yet the worst image of all was the countless innocent dead strewn upon the cold Orkney shores as they had left them a few days ago.

Lucifer was just too strong. Aerling could never win against him. So he gave up. Might as well accept defeat.

"No," he answered at last. "At Hakon, I draw the line." He had to look away when he said it. He just couldn't bear to watch that hope, so trusting, shatter in his brother's eyes.

Magnus also looked away, equally defeated. "Let's drop

Hakon for now," he suggested sadly.

Aerling thought, *I would love to. Straight over a cliff.* But he managed to bite his tongue.

Neither of them could think of anything more to say. Aerling saw Magnus close his eyes again. Whether overcome with exhaustion, or in silent prayer, he couldn't tell. But what he could tell was that his brother was a mess. He needed water and food desperately. Especially the water.

If not, he was going to die. Simple as that.

Aerling felt a sick feeling in his gut. Just seeing his brother like that these last four days was one of the hardest things of his life. Maybe it was time, he suddenly decided, to try to remember a few of those old prayers after all.

Chapter Thirteen

The moment her sister, whom she had been visiting, called Lady Thora with alarm to the window, she realized something was dreadfully wrong. It took only one glance outside at her daughter, riding breakneck speed across the field towards the dwelling, and Thora was seized with an almost irrational panic. Why, Gunnhild never rode like that. She was always so perfectly graceful, so ladylike, and here she was charging at full gallop, her cloak flying wildly behind her, as if she were one of the boys. Whether it was because Thora was the wife of Jarl Erlend and forever braced for violence, or simply because her motherly instinct told her that this was not at all normal, she knew immediately that something terrible had happened. In a flash, she herself was out the door, running across the yard to meet her.

Gunnhild reined in so abruptly that the horse nearly reared beneath her. She leapt to the ground, her eyes wide with horror. Gunnhild was Thora and Erlend's second-born, and as such had already seen more savagery in her short twenty years than other maidens might see in a lifetime. She was usually so calm, taking even bloodshed in stride as a normal part of life. If she was in such a frantic state, Thora knew there was a reason.

"Mother!" she blurted, her voice coming out almost a sob. "The Mainland's been invaded. The news is all over the village."

Thora felt her heart stop.

"Warriors are everywhere! They're pouring over the isle."

Gunnhild was grabbing her mother's arm, propelling her urgently towards the house. "We must hide! They're coming!"

Thora's sister had followed her into the yard. "Who?" she asked, her face draining of color. "Who is coming?"

"The Northmen! King Berrfott's son Sigurd was left here with an army!" Gunnhild turned to Thora and her expression held an anguish her mother had never seen. "Father was captured! And Aerling and Magnus too!"

"Dear God! When, Gunnhild? When did this happen?"

"A few days ago. Five or six. Hurry, Mother." She was pulling Thora across the yard. "Where is Cecily?"

Thora's mind went suddenly blank, as if this were a dream and could not really be happening. She tried to remember where her youngest child was. It was her sister who answered for her.

"Cecily is safe in the house."

They were there now too, at the entrance. Gunnhild was shoving the two older women inside, strangely taking charge. Thora saw her drop the heavy bolt into place and dash straight into the kitchen, where she searched wildly for the largest butcher knife her aunt owned. She would use it too, this daughter of Erlend; of that Thora had no doubt. In her own way, gentle Gunnhild was just as bold as her two brothers when faced with danger. Hardly anyone would ever guess, judging by her fragile, lovely looks, but within the princess beat a heart that knew no fear. She would never yield without a fight.

Yet Thora knew that without her husband or her sons to protect them, the four females locked in this house would be utterly defenseless if the Vikings found them here. What was a kitchen knife, or even an axe from the barn, against the Norsemen? Hardly a more dreaded invader could have landed upon their shores.

But the Jarl's wife knew also that nothing could befall her or her daughters, no evil whatsoever, without the permission of an all-loving God. He was at this very moment with them and would shield them from harm much more securely than even Erlend or Aerling or Magnus could do. That knowledge slowly calmed her, and together with the others, she bent to her knees before the crucifix over the hearth, and stormed Heaven harder than she ever had before.

Chapter Fourteen

Magnus did not even know anymore how long they had been chained down here in the cargo-hold. After the first week, he had stopped even trying to count. With so much suffering to endure, the days had a way of blurring into each other, and the only thing to mark the passing of time was the appearance of the man who brought down their food. The amount King Berrfott allowed was enough to keep them alive, but hardly more. It was not the continual hunger however which Magnus found the hardest to bear. It was the excruciating thirst. Now he understood why the wounded on battlefields always cried out in such agony for water.

But Aerling, of course, realized this, and gave him as much of his own as possible. Their chains did not permit them to actually reach each other, but his brother was able to pass his cup over to where Magnus could take it. There was no point even trying to object; Magnus knew he had more chance of winning an argument with a block of granite than with big brother, especially in a case like this. Yet he also knew that, while it was meritorious and pleasing to God to render charity to someone in need, it was sometimes even more virtuous to accept another's kindness with humility and gratitude. To refuse his brother's heroic self-sacrifice would not only be extremely insulting, but also the height of pride. So Magnus took whatever Aerling insisted on giving him, whether food or drink, and was more grateful than words could ever say.

And to be honest, he did not know how he could bear it otherwise.

But Aerling was tough, tougher than almost anyone Magnus knew, including much more seasoned warriors. It would take an awful lot to wear him down. A few more days and he would be forced to keep more for himself, and eventually all. He was only human. He was also the Orkney's crown-prince and his responsibility towards his vanquished kingdom justly outweighed any personal responsibility he may feel towards keeping his younger brother alive. Although he had not spoken about it, Magnus knew full well that Aerling would attempt an escape at the first chance he got, and for that he could not let himself starve. But for the present, Aerling gave of his water and food with a generosity that could not possibly be surpassed. Yet it cost him. He didn't show it, but Magnus knew it cost him dearly.

Neither of them had any idea where this ship was going or why it was taking so long. It could not be heading to Norway, for they would have been there by now. Their best guess was that Berrfott was raiding other coastlines . . . probably heading to war with Ireland. Everyone knew the young king had been drooling over that piece of dirt since the day he was born.

Magnus vaguely wondered what had happened to Hakon, but he would not dare bring it up. To his shame, he didn't really care. All he cared about was when the man was next going to show up with their water. Less than two weeks of captivity and the Norwegians had already reduced him as low as this. The waiting bordered on torture, every time. Between that and his knee, not even to mention his other wounds, it was hard for Magnus to care about anything else.

He gingerly shifted his position on the floor, an action which always brought fresh bolts of pain. He'd given up even trying to lie down anymore; it was just too hard. He prayed that his brother wouldn't guess how much it all hurt. Aerling had his own problems, plenty of them, and didn't need any more dumped on him. Magnus had been trying so hard to keep his miseries to himself, but he feared he was doing a lousy job.

He found his gaze traveling involuntarily, as it did so often, towards the door at the top of the stairs. *Please God,* he begged, *let there be water soon.*

Aerling must have seen, for he pulled himself out of his own gloomy thoughts and said, "He'll be here soon. Just hang in there, Magnus."

Magnus nodded, ashamed of himself, and forced his eyes away from the door. He was too weak to even answer.

He could tell that Aerling's temper was dangerously on edge. He looked ready to explode. This whole ordeal would be a martyrdom for anyone, but Magnus knew Satan was having a field-day with his poor brother. Hatred for Hakon was simply devouring him. It actually seemed to have festered deeper since their conversation of a few days ago, when Aerling had come so very close to forgiving their cousin, then had rejected the grace in the end. Oh yes, Lucifer was strong. A seraph, after all! He had his victim in a strangle-hold and Magnus wondered how his brother would ever break free of those demonic claws before they brought him to Hell.

Yet there was one creature, he knew, who was stronger than all of the fallen angels combined. She had crushed the infernal serpent's head a million times before and would continue to do so until the end of the world. She loved Aerling's soul more than Magnus did, and she was a Mother, always ready to help. Magnus would not give up asking her, no matter how long it took.

Without meaning to, he went back to staring at the door, as if by sheer willpower he could compel the man to hurry up and come.

All he could think about was water!

"Stop watching for him. It's bad enough without you making it worse for both of us!"

Well, he was certainly doing a magnificent job of hiding his suffering, wasn't he? Magnus again ripped his eyes away from that stupid door. *Offer it up, you useless wimp!* he told himself angrily. *All it is is a little bit of thirst. It won't kill you!*

But it truly felt like it would.

There was only one other thing he could think of, and it was just as bad. If he concentrated on his knee, which wasn't very hard to do, then he could nearly forget his thirst for a few seconds. Pain, water. Water, pain. His mind jumped back and forth between the two torments, ready to drive him insane! It all hurt so much that he didn't dare look across at his brother, lest Aerling see the agony in his eyes. It would only make him hate Hakon more.

Hakon. He was the third pain to think about. Magnus needed to find a way to get Aerling to forgive him! After this voyage, the two of them would probably be separated and who was to say he would ever see his brother again? Magnus had to convince him to forgive their cousin. But *how?* He had tried everything. Reasoning didn't work, and arguing only made it worse. The only thing left was prayer, and he'd been doing that for ages already, especially since Hakon had burned Helge's farm two years ago and had increased Aerling's wrath incredibly. Yes, Magnus had been praying his heart out for his brother. That and penance and begging the Blessed Virgin to intercede. But so far Heaven seemed deaf to all his pleas, while meantime Lucifer was gaining strength in leaps and bounds. What was it going to take to get Heaven to answer? Magnus was willing to do anything, if only he knew what.

"I said, stop staring at that blasted door, will you? You're driving me crazy!"

Magnus hadn't even realized he'd been looking at it this time; it had become such a habit. Oh yes, Aerling was definitely volatile right now. One wrong move and he was really going to explode. Magnus couldn't blame him for being on the brink. His brother was equally deprived of nourishment, and of the little offered him, he denied himself over half with the greatest of valor for Magnus's sake. Aerling may be hard as steel, but he was still human. And it was beginning to show. These last few days, he was starting to look really worn out. For all his toughness, Aerling was suffering greatly too, especially from the thirst. How could he not be? It might be wise, Magnus suddenly decided, to pretend to go to sleep. At least then he couldn't accidentally stare at the door.

Lying down meant more pain, which he couldn't handle, so he leaned back where he was sitting against the wall and closed his eyes. He waited a minute or two until Aerling had hopefully forgotten his existence, then slipped his hand into his blood soaked shirt and took out the little crucifix which he always carried with him. The Norwegians, of course, had stripped him of his chainmail and weapons, but his crucifix and small worn prayerbook of psalms they had not bothered to confiscate. He was much too exhausted to even attempt to read, but he often pressed the crucifix against his heart in silent prayer when his brother wasn't looking. It helped him to be brave, especially by thinking about Christ's tormenting thirst on the Cross. Magnus decided that must have been one of His most frightful tortures, because it was the one thing, the only, that had actually wrung a complaint from the Savior's lips. Now Magnus understood why. How precious souls must be, he realized, to have been bought at such a terrifying price. Somehow these things had taken on a whole new meaning down here.

"Magnus?" Aerling said suddenly.

Magnus opened his eyes and looked over at him. It was hard to even focus. He felt strangely disorientated, as if he might pass out if he didn't soon get some water.

His brother was sitting forward eagerly. "Magnus, what is that?"

"Huh? What is what?" His mouth was so parched it was difficult to even form words.

"Why didn't you tell me you smuggled something in? Maybe we can use it to get out of here!"

What on earth was Aerling talking about?

"Toss it over. Let me see it."

Feeling totally lost, Magnus just looked at him.

"The thing you're holding, dummy! If there's something sharp on it, I might be able to unlock these chains."

Magnus was confused, until he realized Aerling must be talking about the crucifix in his hand. What else could he mean? But ---

"Just throw it over here, will you?"

Magnus hesitated, then automatically obeyed. As gently as he could, he tossed the sacred object across the room.

His brother easily caught it, and that's when the door opened. A sudden shaft of almost blinding sunlight sliced through the room from above, and Food Man started to descend the stairs. Aerling had no time to examine the object in his hand. He just barely managed to shove it beneath the blanket beside him to hide it, and then the Norwegian was standing there in front of them.

Magnus forgot everything else as his eyes locked on one thing only: the jug. The Norseman had brought bread too. Stale dry stuff that was like swallowing gravel each time. Every day Magnus told himself he must eat first and save his water to wash the bread down. To do it the other way around only added to the torture.

But he couldn't help it; he would always reach straight for his cup, draining its entire contents in a few frantic gulps.

That's where his brother's heroism inevitably came to the rescue. But Magnus knew they could not keep going like this. There was going to come a point very soon when Aerling could no longer sacrifice even a portion of his own water or food. Oh yes, he was definitely weakening too.

The Norwegian, as usual, said nothing. Aerling, as usual, did.

"We're going to end up dead if your idiot king refuses to give us more to drink. You *have* to get that across to him. Just look at my poor brother. He's not going to survive long enough to be ransomed!"

The Norseman silently studied Magnus, as if trying to decide how bad those wounds really were. The heavy bloodstains all over his clothes should have been abundant evidence to anyone, but maybe this fellow was exceptionally thick. Giving no indication of his thoughts, he finally turned to leave.

By unspoken agreement, neither of Erlend's sons would ever reach for anything until the man was gone. They would not give him the pleasure of seeing how desperate they were. After all, they were princes despite everything and were entitled to some last shred of dignity.

But the second the door had closed behind him, Magnus flew for his cup. He was so desperate by now that his hands were trembling. Aerling likewise did not waste a single moment. In his own need for food and drink, he had completely forgotten about the object shoved so hastily beneath his blanket on the floor.

Magnus was shaking so badly he nearly spilled the precious contents as he tried to raise the cup to his lips. He was just about to gulp down the life-saving water when, suddenly, in the depths of his soul, he distinctly heard a Voice.

Sitio, It pleaded.

Magnus froze, startled. The cup was still held half way to his mouth.

He knew that word from the Gospel. It was Latin and it meant, *I thirst.* The Son of God had uttered it in agony from His throne of the Cross. He thirsted for souls. Souls of sinners.

Immediately and with perfect clarity, Magnus understood what his Divine Master was asking of him. Make the sacrifice of this drink of water to win for his brother the grace of conversion. Had not Christ said elsewhere in the Gospel that certain devils could be cast out by nothing but fasting? Aerling was obviously caught in the stronghold of a demon of that ilk; his hatred for Hakon was destroying him. If someone didn't help, it was unlikely he would save his immortal soul.

The realization of what God was asking of him was terrifying and Magnus was seized with something close to panic. His first thought was to ignore it, pretend he had not heard that imploring Voice. He had told God over and over again that he was willing to do anything, *anything* it took, to get Aerling to forgive Hakon. But *this?* How could he? He was so tormented with thirst that he felt he would surely die.

God, please, he thought wildly, *I can't! Anything else. Not this!*

With the same perfect clarity as the first thought had come, a second immediately rose up within him. Go to that ever-merciful Mother, who loved souls so much that she had undergone martyrdom at the foot of her Son's Cross. She would help; she would be right here with all the graces Magnus needed to endure this penance. *Do it for Aerling, lest he end up in Hell,* she seemed to be saying.

Slowly, dreadfully, his heart pounding with sudden violence,

Magnus lowered the cup and placed it on the floor. So, that was the incredible bargain he was apparently making with Heaven. Nothing to drink, not one single drop, until Aerling forgave their cousin.

Dear God, this was going to be Purgatory.

"Magnus?" Aerling asked, baffled. "Why aren't you drinking anything?"

Magnus was caught off-guard. It had never occurred to him that his brother might be watching. He didn't know what to say.

Aerling's confusion rapidly gave way to alarm.

"Hey, what's wrong with you?" In the short space that Magnus had been sitting here doing nothing, his brother had already wolfed down his own food and water, the amount he would take of them, and had slid the remainder over to within Magnus's reach.

For the first time since their capture, he shook his head in refusal and made no move to accept.

Aerling was staring at him like he was crazy. "Take it," he ordered, but his voice faltered slightly, as if he somehow sensed he was suddenly up against something he could not control. "What's gotten into you? Drink something!"

There was no way he could let Aerling know the reason. His brother would just have to make of it what he wanted. Magnus had to violently tear his gaze away from the two cups of water waiting beside him, unable to even bear seeing them there. He couldn't help it; he started to tremble almost uncontrollably --- not only with the agonizing thirst itself, but also with the intensity of the struggle not to give in. Pulling his blanket quickly around him in a helpless attempt to hide his shuddering, he buried himself in desperate prayer.

"Magnus, talk to me. What's going on?"

Say nothing. Ignore him. Don't even look at him!

"Magnus, I'm ordering you!"

Forgive Hakon, Magnus implored him silently. *God, please make Satan leave my poor brother alone!*

Wrapping his arms tightly around himself trying to stop the violent trembling, Magnus turned his thoughts to Christ on the Cross and His Mother beneath it, and prayed with more heartfelt fervor than he had ever done in all his nineteen years.

Chapter Fifteen

The trip to Norway had been, for Jarl Paal, a living nightmare. That was the only way to describe it. The actual journey had not taken long, only a couple of days, but once the ship reached Norwegian shores, he had been dragged from one place to another, first this fortress then that, as the enemy tried to decide, in the absence of their king, just where the two Orkney Jarls should go.

After their initial capture, Paal had been separated from his brother Erlend, and for that he was grateful. He could never have faced the other Jarl, *never,* once the deplorable truth had come out. His son whom he loved so much, his very own boy Hakon, had been the one behind the massacre and had caused the downfall of their kingdom. The knowledge was painful and humiliating beyond words, but at least Paal had not witnessed his brother's reaction. To see Erlend's wrath would have been more than he could bear.

So, here Paal now was, flanked by two armed warriors, his hands tied behind his back, as they shoved him along through the dark subterranean corridor. Somehow he sensed this was it, his final destination. His own child, flesh of his flesh and blood of his blood, had condemned him for the rest of his life to a dungeon. *Oh Hakon,* he thought over and over again, *How could you? How could you?* Paal's heart ached so much he felt like he was suffocating with the grief.

The Norwegians halted before a cell and in the light from their burning torch the Jarl could see it was criss-crossed with heavy steel bars. As one of them swung open the iron door, the other savagely pushed Paal through it, so roughly that he stumbled and fell to the floor. With his wrists bound so tightly behind him, he could hardly get back up. He felt the perspiration pouring down him as he struggled clumsily to regain his feet; he could almost taste the fear in his mouth. What were they going to do to him now that he was here? He had already afforded the Norsemen plenty of sport in the days past. He didn't think he could take any more humiliation.

To his relief, one of the guards untied his hands. They were numb and he rubbed and shook them vigorously, trying to bring the feeling back. The two men were leaving now, clanging the door shut behind them. He heard the key click in the heavy lock, and the Vikings left, taking the torch, the only source of light, with them.

Paal was alone in the pitch dark.

Shakily, he groped around in the blackness, trying to get his bearings. In that instant before they had pushed him to the floor, he had spotted a board with what might be blankets . . . It must be their idea of a bed. Well, he was lucky. He might not have had one at all. With caution he moved in the direction he believed it might be in, until he bumped into it and gratefully sank down. He buried his face in his hands. There were no tears left. *Oh Hakon, oh Hakon, you stupid boy! How could you?*

How long he remained there on the bed, exhausted and broken, he had no idea. It may have been an hour, it may have been more. He was numb with sorrow. The darkness surrounding him was absolute, the only sound a distant drip-dripping of water somewhere. Occasionally he heard a few scraping noises, probably rats. He realized his heart was tightened in his chest, his breath was coming hard. He felt almost in shock.

Then, slowly, he became aware of a new noise. There was a commotion of some sort down the corridor. He lifted his head and strained to listen. A door clanged far away, voices echoed in the darkness. He heard distant footsteps; then they came closer. Whoever the party was, they must have turned a corner because suddenly a faint glow of torchlight became visible. Paal stood up and made his way to the bars to look out. He felt like his legs might give way beneath him and he held on to the cold iron for support.

The flame of the torch was coming nearer, making shadows leap crazily across the blackened stone walls. He could see three men making their way through the underground passage and he recognized two of them as the same guards who had brought him down. The third was obviously another prisoner, and he looked in even worse shape than Paal. Blood streaked the man's face and clothing; he was hobbling along pitifully and once or twice tripped and fell, only to be yanked ruthlessly back to his feet by the others.

Paal should have known whom the newcomer would be, but for some reason he did not recognize him in the dark, covered as he was with so much filth and blood. It was not until the guards pulled the wretched prisoner to a stop directly in front of Paal's cage that he found himself face to face with his brother.

Dear God, he thought with horror, *what have they done to him?*

Paal wanted to look away; he tried, but one of the Norsemen reached through the bars and grabbed a fistful of his hair, savagely jerking his face back towards his brother.

Erlend's eyes blazed and for a terrible moment Paal was sure he would rip free of the guards' restraining hold and himself reach through those bars to smash Paal's face in. Instinctively Paal leapt back out of the way, then he realized that Erlend's hands were bound behind his back. A surge of relief swept over him. His brother could not reach him in here, could not do anything to hurt him.

Amused, one of the guards asked, "Either of you have anything to say? Any loving words of farewell between brothers? Because if you do, say them now. It's the last chance you shall ever get."

Paal lowered his eyes to the floor, shame burning through him. He braced himself for the tirade of abuse that his brother would no doubt let fly, knowing that whatever insults Erlend hurled at him would all be just and true. Hakon had gone way too far, and Paal could not blame the other Jarl if he hated the father who had bred and reared such a Judas.

But . . . incredibly . . . when his brother spoke, it was not the abuse Paal was expecting. Fighting to control the rage in his voice, Erlend manged to get out four words. They were the last Paal would ever hear him speak.

"I forgive your son."

Paal looked up, startled, and for the briefest of seconds their eyes met.

Then, before he could think of any reply, the guards thrust his brother away from the heavy steel bars and continued their way down the dungeon corridor, taking the last light with them.

The two sons of Thorfinn the Mighty would never see each other again.

Chapter Sixteen

Aerling was at wits end. He simply could not believe his brother was doing this. What in the wide world was going on? It had been hours ago, when, completely out of the blue, Magnus had launched some kind of a hunger strike. It was bizarre. No, worse --- it was downright frightening. Didn't the little idiot realize how crucial water was in his near-critical condition? Aerling had never been so worried in his life.

The strangest part of all was that Magnus refused to tell him why. He had simply pushed aside both water and food, wrapped himself up in some inaccessible refuge of prayer, and would not say a word. It was not in a spirit of defiance; he wasn't trying to prove a point or win an argument, or anything like that. No, Aerling could tell that whatever was going on, it was not intended as a battle of wills.

What then? Was he doing this as a penance? That was the type of pious stunt he *would* have to pull, but why now of all times? And why in something so serious? As if he didn't have plenty to offer up already! Aerling was just about frantic trying to figure out what to do with him.

The irony of the situation was unbelievable. After almost two weeks of captivity, Aerling had at last, mere hours ago, penetrated the thick skull of that brain-dead Norwegian who brought their food, and had convinced him, *finally,* to relay his message to the king. As a result, Berrfott had relented of his harshness, obviously preferring the gold of ransom to corpses in his ship's hull, and had sent Deadhead back down with more food. So here they sat, no longer with rock-hard bread on the floor between them, but with things actually meant for human consumption, not even to mention a few brimming jugs of water. Aerling himself had felt no guilt in taking his fill, and there was still plenty left for his brother. Surely Magnus would start recovering if only he would eat. He was young and he was tough; even with those wounds, Aerling knew he could still regain his strength. Yet now that the vital nourishment had arrived, Magnus refused to touch them. Good grief.

The light was fading as evening came on, and darkness would be a blessed relief. Aerling couldn't stand it anymore, watching his brother suffer like that. He sat back against the wall and tried to think if Magnus had said anything in these last few days which might explain why he was doing this to himself. There had to be a reason. He wasn't doing it for nothing!

So, what had they talked about? Not much, actually. Magnus spent most of the time drifting in and out of that strange sleep, which Aerling suspected bordered on semi-unconsciousness, and when he was awake, he was in so much pain that he didn't feel like talking. Which had suited Aerling just fine, because he'd been in a foul temper himself and the less said the better. In fact, it was much easier to recall all the things they had *not* talked about, rather than the few things they had.

Escape, for example. That had not been mentioned even once. Magnus surely must know that he would try to bolt the first chance that came, but not for the world was Aerling going to discuss it with him. To abandon his younger brother, wounded and half-dead in enemy hands, hardly able to walk, was going to be the hardest thing of Aerling's life. But, as their father's heir, he felt he had no choice but to try to escape if he could. Besides, after this voyage they would certainly be separated; Magnus would end up on his own anyhow.

Another subject they had carefully avoided was their family. Neither of them had any inclination to talk about the horrors which were doubtless in store for their father in Norway. Nor did it pay to contemplate their mother and two sisters back home. All too painful. They both kept it locked inside.

What then *had* they talked about? Aerling realized with shame that most of what they said to each other had deteriorated into arguing. Hakon, of course, was the sole reason for that. The slime wasn't even aboard this ship, yet he still managed to barge his way between them, causing every argument they had. He'd been doing it for the last two years!

Well, whatever. Obviously Hakon had nothing whatsoever to do with Magnus's all-but-suicidal fast.

Usually the mere thought of their cousin was enough to put Aerling on the boil, but for some reason he was too tired right now to even care. He knew he had zero chance of getting any sleep, not with Magnus such a wreck over there, but he was so drained that he decided he might as well at least lie down.

First, however, he would give it one more try.

"Magnus," he said wearily, "listen to me."

To his surprise, his brother actually looked over. His eyes showed such intensity of suffering that Aerling almost wished he hadn't. But there was something else in them as well. A silent desperate pleading, as if Magnus were begging him to do something. But what? Aerling didn't understand.

"You have to stop this," he said. "I really mean that, Magnus. You have no right, none whatsoever, to kill yourself! Do you understand me? *You're going to kill yourself!"*

For the first time in all these terrible hours, Magnus spoke. Or at least tried to. He was so weakened he could barely talk at all, but he somehow managed a couple words.

"You . . . kill . . ."

He had to pause; the effort seemed beyond his strength. Aerling knew his thirst by now, together with all that pain, must be beyond endurance. Small wonder he could hardly speak. When he was able to continue, Aerling had to strain to catch each word.

"You kill . . . your immortal soul . . . and . . . think . . . nothing of it."

The reproach was so unexpected that at first it didn't even register. Aerling just stared at him, confused. Why would his brother say something like that, and now of all times? Magnus was referring, of course, to mortal sin. That much was obvious. But what had that to do with his refusal to drink? The two didn't fit together.

Or . . . did they?

The incredible realization struck Aerling with the force of a sudden punch in the gut. Could his brother be doing this for . . . *him?*

He was too stunned to even react.

For a minute he just sat there, looking at his brother with disbelief. Did Magnus really love him *that much* to do such a frightening penance to save his soul? For Aerling understood suddenly without a doubt that that's what it was. It was exactly the sort of thing his saintly little brother would do. Why hadn't he figured it out before? It was suddenly so obvious! With a feeling very near to physical sickness, and knowing he had no reply, Aerling reached for his blanket to lie down. After all, what could he possibly say?

It was when he pulled the blanket towards him that the object hidden beneath was uncovered. So preoccupied had he been with this whole situation that he'd actually forgotten about the thing which Magnus hours ago had tossed over to him. He had hoped at the time that, whatever it was, he might be able to use it as a tool to unlock their chains. Now, in the fading light, he picked it up to examine it.

It was a crucifix.

He wasn't quite sure what he had expected, but it wasn't this. Yet what else would his brother have smuggled in? It made perfect sense, of course. But for some reason it still took Aerling by surprise to find such an object held in his hand. For a moment he looked at it, his heart sinking with disappointment. No, there was no way he could pick the locks with this thing. It was useless.

He was about to discard it, to put it back on the floor, when Magnus's words of a few days ago came, unbidden, to his mind.

Oh sure, God is cruel alright. Cruel to the point of being crucified for each and every one of us! Is that your idea of cruel? Dying for someone you love?

Magnus would die for him. Aerling knew that now. Actually, deep down, he had always known it, just as he had always known he would give his own life, if necessary, for his brother. But he had never believed, *truly believed,* that God could love him with such a staggering love. Was it true? Had the One on the cross, over a thousand years ago, actually hung there for him? Honestly for *him,* to pay the ransom for his soul? The catechism had told him that. The monks of Eynhallow had told him that. A whole lifetime of boring Sunday sermons, most of which he had yawned through, had all held the same message. God loved him, Aerling Erlendson personally, and had become a Man living and toiling and suffering on this same planet earth for the simple reason to die for his sins. *His* sins, each and every one of them, and they were more numerous than Aerling could count. Yet God Himself had paid the debt, *had already handed over the ransom money!*

He didn't understand where these thoughts, so very foreign to him, were coming from, nor why he suddenly didn't want to put the crucifix down. But for a long time he silently looked at it in the last of the fading light, and wondered how it was possible that he had spent his whole life giving almost no thought, and certainly very little love, to One Who had willfully accepted much greater thirst and incomparably more pain than even his heroic little brother was enduring for him. If Magnus loved him so much to make such a sacrifice to save his soul, how much greater must be the love of a Crucified God! It all but took his breath away.

He could not explain it, nor even less understand its source, but as Aerling gazed at the crucifix in his hand, something amazing rose up inside him, an inexplicable yearning unlike anything he had ever felt before. He suddenly wanted to love this God back.

"Magnus?" he said impulsively.

It was too dark now to see his brother, but of course he was still awake.

"Can God really pardon me after all I've done? I mean, aren't my sins too many to be forgiven?" It was something he would never say, never even *dream* of saying to anyone, except maybe to a priest in a confessional. Yet here he was, blurting out such an intimate question to his little brother in the darkness of an enemy cargo-hold somewhere in the North Sea. And suddenly he wished more than anything that he could have one more chance to kneel in that box he had been avoiding for years.

It took nearly a full minute for Magnus to even comprehend

the words he had spoken, let alone be able to reply. It was a miracle he could manage to speak at all.

"God will . . . forgive anything, Aerling. If . . . you do."

Right. It came back, as always, to the same thing.

Forgive us our trespasses as we forgive those . . .

"I forgive Hakon."

The words just tumbled out.

A stunned silence dropped like mortar. Neither of them could believe what he had just said. Aerling didn't know who was the more flabbergasted, himself or his brother. But what he did know was that an unimaginable peace, beyond anything he had ever experienced, instantly flooded through his heart.

There was a rattling of chains and he knew that Magnus had sat suddenly forward. *"What . . . ?"* he gasped, as if unsure he had heard right.

"I said, I forgive him." It came out so easily, and as he spoke those five simple little words, the peace in his heart soared into a profound and indescribable joy.

Then he heard, to his unspeakable relief, the sound of a cup scraping across the floor in the darkness as his brother reached with pure desperation for the water that would save his life. And, for the first time ever, Aerling Erlendson understood perfectly the stupendous *'no greater love'* of the Gospel.

Chapter Seventeen

Ofeig was actually starting to enjoy this life of adventure on the high seas and wished Hakon would stop spoiling all his fun. Now that they had been finally untied by the crew and put to work, this was the sort of things dreams were made of. Blood and battles, midnight raids, close shaves with death. Oh the spellbinding tales he could someday weave around a campfire as an old battle-scarred warrior --- they would be fantastic.

As Ofeig stirred the cauldron of slop which would serve as breakfast for a horde of hungry men, he pictured the scene perfectly in his mind. There he would sit by a crackling fire, a venerable elder, surrounded by eager young faces all turned to him with awe. He would show them his impressive scars and all would gasp in admiration. "Back in the days of yore," he would say, "when I was but a young sprog, I sailed with the legendary King Berrfott of Norway." Again, more gasps and ahh's. "Together we fought, side by side, on the shores of the Hebrides. I was the one who captured their prince, a giant of a Viking named Logmann Godrodarson whom none dared take on in battle but I and the king."

Ofeig liked his story. It didn't actually matter that his scars were the result of falling off his pony and landing on a sharp rock when he was eleven years old, nor that his one brief glimpse of Berrfott had been while waiting outside the door in the castle while Hakon convinced the young king to attack the Orkneys. No, no, those were minor details and did not affect his tale at all.

The important thing was . . . he was *here*! In the midst of a conquest that would change the course of Scandinavian history and go down in song and legend. So what if Logmann Godrodarson was a scrawny, squat man and that the only part Ofeig had played in the great battle was sitting at the ship's oars with Hakon, then mopping the blood off the deck afterward? Things were bound to get better, after all. He had already made friends with most of the crew and frequently shared a horn of mead with them in the evenings. There were even rumors floating about that because of the heavy losses the Norwegians had sustained in the Hebrides, Berrfott was now desperately short of men. He was going to need more warriors. If Ofeig played his hand right, he might find a sword in it at the next battle.

Yes, all in all, Ofeig's future was looking bright. He didn't care which leader he followed. An Orkney Jarl, a Norwegian king, all were the same to him. What he lived for was adventure. And heading to war with Ireland held more promise of that in a single week than in a lifetime on the boring Orkneys. The most daring escapade he had ever been involved in *there* was burning a ramshackle cottage to the ground and helping gag a gorgeous girl, which were Hakon's little ideas to spite his cousin on his other side. It had worked beautifully. Too beautifully in fact. Both those crimes had been done against Ofeig's better judgment. After all, the absolute *last* person Ofeig cared to have for an enemy was Aerling Erlendson. Talk about suicide! Even Sihvat and Gurd Sock were wary of Aerling, yet they'd take on Lucifer himself. It was only fools like Hakon who crossed Aerling on purpose.

Well, all four of them had escaped with their lives after the debacle at Helge Stianson's farm. Incredibly, even Hakon still had body and soul hanging together, yet how he had pulled that miracle, Ofeig still didn't know. Probably Hakon didn't either. It was mind-boggling that he had walked --- or to be more exact, lurched --- out of that Assembly Hall two years ago actually alive. All Ofeig knew was that after that day, Hakon's neck had displayed some rather interesting marks for quite some time. Ofeig always regretted he hadn't been there to see what had actually happened. It would have been spectacular to watch. But he had been too scared about his own neck to slip into the Council that day!

At least Aerling wasn't on this boat. He was somewhere out there, along with his brother, but the fleet was big and Ofeig hoped he would never have to face either of Erlend's sons again after what had just happened in the Orkneys. If Hakon had a brain anywhere in his head, he would be thinking the same thoughts too.

Speaking of Hakon, Ofeig glanced up past the cauldron and spotted his cousin across the warship's kitchen --- if kitchen was the right word. Hakon was viciously ripping up chunks of bread to dole out with Ofeig's slop to the hungry warriors, his face set in an ugly scowl.

"Hmm. I wonder what I can use to flavor this soup," Ofeig said loudly. All perfectly innocent, of course. "You know, make it a bit more tasty. Nothing like a nice stew on a cold day." He paused, pretending to think. "Say, cous, can I have a few locks of your hair?"

Hakon looked up savagely.

Ofeig grinned and began to hum a little tune he been composing over the last several days. He even had words for it. Well, some words. He started to sing. Quietly, but just loud enough that Hakon would overhear.

> "There once was a woman,
> gorgeous as can be.
> The future of anyone
> she could surely see.

The menu of the day
just happened to be stew.
She clawed a chunk of princely hair,
and dumped it ---"

And that's where Ofeig always got stuck. He couldn't think of anything appropriate to rhyme with stew. Snare rhymed with hair, but that didn't work either.

Across the room his cousin pierced him with a murderous look.

Ofeig gave him his most charming smile and continued singing his merry song.

Chapter Eighteen

Kol Kalison had not yet met his king's hostages, but, like the rest of Scandinavia, he knew Jarl Erlend's sons by reputation. Had it not been for that, the young Norwegian nobleman might have brought down their weapons himself, as Berrfott had told him to do. But these two were fighters, exceptional fighters, and Kol wasn't going to take any foolish risks. Leave that to the armorer. Kol Kalison wanted to live.

He opened the door to the cargo-hold and looked down the stairs, holding his lantern in front of him. There wasn't much light down there. After over three weeks their eyes would be adjusted to the dimness, but his weren't. He was immediately appalled by the dampness and stench which rose up to meet him; he'd automatically assumed King Berrfott would imprison the pair in a more respectable place than this! After all, these two princes were worth a small fortune. But the inexperienced monarch, even younger than Kol himself, was like that---cruel to the point of serious imprudence. At least, Kol thought to himself, they were still alive and could hopefully be used. Because, frankly, Norway was desperate.

He descended the stairs two at a time, aware of their hostile gazes upon him. This had to be quick, no mincing of words. The Welsh were out there and the first sounds of sea-battle could be heard in the distance. Surely the Orkney captives could hear it too.

"You two," Kol ordered without preamble, "get to your feet.

There's work for you above deck."

They looked first at him, then at each other. Neither moved a muscle. It was clear they had no intention whatsoever to obey.

"Who," one of them asked coldly, "on earth are you?"

"My name is Kol Kalison. King Berrfott sent me to unchain you. Stand up and I'll get those shackles off. You first."

Now most men, Kol would imagine, would leap at the chance of being released. Not this one. The Orkney prince merely glowered at him and demanded, "Why?"

Kol thought, this *has* to be Aerling, the eldest. Kol had heard all about him and his attitude problem.

"Because," he answered sarcastically, "I said so." To add a little gentle emphasis, he gave him a swift kick in the gut.

He heard the prisoner draw in a sharp breath of pain, but it certainly convinced him to rise to his feet as told. Aerling got up, yet with deliberate slowness, obviously meant to defy. He said nothing, not one single word, but his eyes were steel. As if accepting a challenge, he deigned to hold out his wrists for Kol to unlock the manacles. His expression seemed to say, *Go ahead, Kol. Make my day.*

All of a sudden, Kol changed his mind. Let the younger brother unchain this one, when he himself was out of the pit. Kol was armed to the teeth, but even so, he didn't really want to be down here alone with an uncaged tiger.

Hoping Aerling wouldn't guess his true reason, which of course would amount to paying him the ultimate compliment, Kol turned to the second son of Jarl Erlend and said, "Let's just leave your sibling to stew a bit longer, shall we? You get up. I'll do you first."

Aerling said, "My brother is too injured to rise."

The young Norseman could already see that. "Then I guess I

shall have to help him up too, won't I?"

"Kick him like you kicked me, and you'll never eat another breakfast in your life."

"Don't worry about me, Aerling," the younger one said. "I can stand." He somehow managed to get up, although Kol could see it was not easy and cost him a lot of pain. Small wonder, judging from all that blood which had soaked through his clothes. Kol was no monster; he'd had no intention whatsoever of hurting this one. He would simply have given him a hand to rise to his feet . . . the real way. In fact, Kol felt sorry for him. Anyone could see the younger prince had been badly wounded before his capture and was obviously in a very weakened state. If anything it angered Kol that Berrfott had left him like this. But in that regard Kol was helpless. He was only down here to obey orders. He went to unchain him, but did it as gently as he could.

"You must be Prince Magnus?"

The other nodded. He leaned against the wall for some support. He also said nothing. Both Orkney princes were looking at Kol with no trace of friendliness. He knew he was the enemy, but it wasn't his fault.

"Why," Aerling demanded a second time, "are you setting us free?" Defiance simply oozed from this one. Kol didn't like him. Not one bit.

"Free?" he replied. "Don't flatter yourself, Erlendson. I've been instructed to set you loose, but believe me, you are nowhere near free."

"Alright then, mighty Kol Whoeverson, why are you setting us loose?"

The young nobleman tried to maintain his dignity. How could he admit this and still pretend his country was strong? His inexperienced king really had messed up. "The Welsh," he answered carefully, "have spotted our warships and have sent their own fleet to block our passage. Looks like we're going to have to fight our way across these waters."

"Which waters? Where are we?"

Kol really wished he hadn't asked that. He didn't want to tell them. It was demeaning and made Norway look like a bunch of fools. Reluctantly he said, "The Menai."

As he expected, his answer was met with a baffled silence. It took a second to sink in, but when it did both sons of Erlend just stared at him with utter disbelief.

"The . . . Menai?" Aerling repeated. "Surely you can't mean the *Strait* of Menai? Are you making this up?"

Kol's stony silence must have said it all.

"How on *earth*," Aerling blurted, too stunned to even sound proud, "did your fleet end up in the Menai Strait?" He turned to his brother and quipped, "These brainless Norwegians couldn't navigate a washbasin."

The younger prince was trying not to laugh. Whether out of courtesy, or simply because it would hurt too much, Kol wasn't sure. But he could tell both brothers found this not only unbelievable, but hilarious. And from their point of view, so might have he. But he couldn't show them that!

"It's none of your bloody business," he snapped, "how we ended up here. The fact is, King Berrfott is short of men. We need you two to help."

His answer only made things worse.

"Your king expects us to *help* him?"

"Isn't that what I just said?" It wasn't easy to remain civil with this one. Kol dangled the key in front of his face and tempted, "Do you want to be unchained or not? It's up to you."

"That would bring the sunshine back into my life no end."

Yes, definitely a dangerous one. Now Kol had the problem of getting out of here first. He didn't trust these two one bit and was staggered that Berrfott was doing this. Well, they were the king's problem, not his.

"I'm needed urgently above deck," he told them, which was true. He tossed the key as casually as he could to the younger prince and said, "I'll leave you to unlock your brother. Then get up the stairs and the armorer will give you your swords."

That really did it.

"You mean . . . we get our *WEAPONS* back?" Aerling was gaping at him as if Kol had just landed from somewhere beyond the stars. Maybe they thought they were being asked to row the boat, or shine the king's shield or something.

"We need warriors," Kol said. "Simple as that."

Even the quiet one was staring at him and his eyes seemed to say, *Your king must be the stupidest man ever born.*

Aerling turned to his brother and asked, "Am I hearing this right, Magnus? They're setting us free --- uh, excuse me, loose --- aboard this ship and actually arming us. You know, giving us stuff custom-designed to maim and kill. Does this sound, um, normal to you? Or is it just me?"

Despite the obvious pain, Magnus managed to joke back, "About as normal as getting a fleet of warships stuck in a channel no wider than a footpath. We really have to hand it to them, Aerling. These Norwegians certainly have some highly developed and unusual talents. Credit where it's due."

Kol was getting fed up. He wasn't the one who had made this blunder. "Don't be so smug, you two," he told them coldly. "King Berrfott may be desperate for these few hours, but he's no fool."

As one, both princes raised their eyebrows as it to say, *Oh really?*

118

"If either of you," Kol continued, "turn your sword against even one of our crew, your father will be executed in Norway. And knowing our men back home, his death won't be a pretty one, I can assure you."

Instantly the prisoners didn't find it so very funny anymore. Even Aerling finally shut his mouth.

"On the other hand," Kol continued, "if you fight well, you will win the king's favor and secure his leniency in your own regard. He bids me tell you that you would be wise to defend this ship to the best of your ability, lest you incur for yourselves further punishment." He wasn't sure himself what more Berrfott would do to punish them. Wasn't this cargo-hold bad enough?

Aerling stated the obvious. "My brother can hardly move. How is he expected to fight?"

Good question. Kol was wondering the same thing.

But it was Magnus himself who calmly answered, "It makes no difference whether or not I can fight, because I won't. Tell your king that if he was stupid enough to get his ships trapped where they don't belong, then the Welsh have every right to block this fleet and defend their shores. Don't even bother returning my sword, because I refuse to help slaughter innocent men."

For some reason, Kol felt compelled to warn him. "My king is not distinguished for his mercy. In fact, I doubt he even knows what the word means. I would not displease him, Prince Magnus, if I were you. He won't hesitate to have you tortured."

The prince bravely answered, "Then so be it. I will not bear arms against the Welsh."

Kol was stunned. And deeply impressed. In that single instant, Magnus had won his respect. Even more, his admiration. But the young Norseman would keep that to himself. Out loud he merely remarked, "Looks like the youngest prince of Orkney is going to prove a troublemaker."

Aerling said, "Leave my brother to me. He'll do what I tell him."

Kol had no idea what that would be. Whatever Aerling was thinking, he hid his thoughts well. But Kol had done his duty down here, so he simply said, "Then tell him to unlock your shackles as soon as I'm above deck, and get up there yourselves. At this rate, the armorer will be an old man by the time you two show up."

He looked at the Orkney hostages one last time, knowing that unless the younger one accepted a sword, he could not possibly survive. This was going to be a bloodbath. Wounded or not, he would have to fight in self-defense, simply to preserve his own life, because once those Welshmen boarded this ship, there would be nowhere to hide. Maybe the older brother could convince him of that.

Kol wondered what the outcome would be, but he really did have urgent things to do. The commotion out there was rising to a frantic pitch; things were moving fast and any second now this deadly battle was going to be on top of them.

Leaving the hostages on their own, Kol Kalison turned and raced up the stairs to face whatever resistance Wales had sent them.

Chapter Nineteen

"He's gone," Aerling said, stunned. "Unlocked you and left, just like that."

Magnus limped painfully over and freed him as well. "This is it, Aerling . . . your chance to escape." He could not have sounded more excited, as if it were he himself who was the one about to get away.

Aerling couldn't believe the opportunity had come upon him so easily. This was better than his wildest dreams. Yet now that the reality was here, he realized that he had never been so torn all in his life. How could he actually abandon his brother, wounded and still so weakened by all that he had been through? The king had increased their rations this last week and a half, and Magnus was slowly regaining a little strength, but he was still far from being his old self.

Aerling's hesitation must have bewildered him because he asked, "You are going to try, aren't you? You'll never get a more perfect chance."

"I can't leave you here alone. I . . . I just can't do that, Magnus."

"You have to. There's no way in the world I can swim to shore, or even to a Welsh boat. Do it, Aerling. You must. Our people back home need you."

Whatever was happening out there, it was starting to sound really wild. Any minute now there would be no place on this ship that was safe. Not even down here. Aerling knew he had to decide, and quickly.

"But what if they punish you for my escape? You heard what that Kol fellow said. The king won't hesitate to torture you."

"He can do nothing to me which God does not allow. Besides, not one man will be able to prove you weren't thrown overboard in battle, like dozens of others. No one will ever know you jumped, except me, and I'm certainly not telling. Those half-witted cavemen will never suspect otherwise."

"But what are *you* going to do? Look at yourself. You can barely walk. I can't abandon you like this, Magnus. You know I can't. You'll be slaughtered within the first five minutes of fighting."

"And if I am, will it make any difference whether or not you are on this ship? We will each die when we are meant to, Aerling, in exactly the way God has ordained from eternity. There is nothing we can do to add one day, nor even one single moment, to the time allotted us by our Creator. If I'm meant to live, He will protect me, yet if I die with innocent blood upon my sword, I will have condemned my own soul to Hell."

Aerling knew in his heart that Magnus was right. To murder even one Welshman would be a mortal sin, nor could either of them fight their real enemy, the Norsemen, lest they sign their father's death-warrant. Magnus had meant every word of what he had said to Kol. This battle was unjust; the Welsh were only defending their country, their waters, their women and their children, exactly as they themselves had done a few weeks ago against this same invading army. Magnus would not raise his sword against anyone, whether Welsh or Norwegian, not even to save his own life. And deep down, Aerling could not have been more proud of him. His little brother was braver by far than the toughest warrior the Orkneys had ever bred.

"You two," an angry voice shouted down at them from above. "Get up here. We haven't got all day."

It must be the armorer, waiting to return their weapons.

"Get off this boat, Aerling. You have to. Stop thinking about what might happen to me. I could not be in safer hands than in God's."

For the first time in his life, Aerling felt the hot sting of tears in his eyes. He tried to blink them back before his brother could see. "I'll raise your ransom, Magnus. I mean that. I'll get that money if it kills me."

"I know you will."

There was nothing left to say.

Aerling moved over to lend his brother a hand, and together they headed up the stairs.

* * * * * *

The instant they made it onto the deck, Magnus could see that Kol was right. The Norwegian fleet was in trouble. Big trouble. Men were running everywhere, shouting orders, doing all the urgent things warriors did in those last desperate moments before battle. It was chaos.

The armorer was all but fuming. "What took you two so long?" he demanded as soon as they appeared at the top of the stairs.

"I had to help my brother. You try climbing those steps with your knee sliced in half. I'd love to see just how quickly you could go." Even as Aerling said it, Magnus could see his gaze swiftly roaming the deck for the easiest escape route. He would have to move fast and they both knew it. No second chances today. Make it or die trying.

The armorer was unsheathing their swords. "Hurry. Take

your weapons." Aerling didn't need urging. He grabbed both and shoved one into his brother's hand, keeping the other for himself. Magnus could see he was preparing to bolt as soon as the right moment came. The armor was saying, "Our king has no choice but to trust you two. Your father's life is in your hands because if either of you betray ---"

His voice was suddenly drown out by an ominous sound which every warrior recognized all too well and the sky was instantly darkened with the flight of a thousand arrows. Magnus heard screams of *"Take cover!"* as men everywhere scrambled for safety, grappling for their heavy wooden shields. He felt Aerling shove him urgently and he dived behind the only thing he could reach, a barrel which had been overturned in the stampede of panicked Norwegians. And just in time too. The deadly rainfall was starting to pour down. He crouched behind it helplessly as the deadly darts drummed down all around him, the sound mixed with the agonized shrieks of those not as lucky to find a place to hide.

A second volley of arrows was soaring now across the sky, launched from the Welsh boats at sea. Huddled behind his pathetic shelter, Magnus caught a glimpse of the armorer as an arrow swooped and embedded itself straight through the man's chest. He let out a terrible cry and Magnus watched as his body contorted and fell. Then he was limp, dead. One of countless already. Just like that.

Finally the lethal shower subsided and Magnus heard the inevitable cry --- the one that Aerling, wherever he was, would be waiting for. "They're boarding the ship! They're boarding the ship!" The news went out and was taken up by others until it rang loud across the deck. The Welsh archers had done their grisly work, now they were diving into the waters and scrabbling up the sides of the Norwegian boats. Magnus thought in his heart, *Run, Aerling! Hurry! Jump overboard!*

Painfully he staggered to his feet and looked around. Welsh shafts littered the ship's floor; carnage was everywhere and the battle had hardly started. It was down now to hand-to-hand, axe, mace and sword. Where was his brother?

Aerling was nowhere to be seen. He must have already made a run for it. *Please God,* Magnus begged, *let him make it.*

A loneliness he had not expected swept over him like a torrent. He was on his own now, truly alone, and suddenly it hurt more than he would ever have believed. But no, he corrected himself, he was not alone. God was with him. And with Aerling too. He would care for them both; how could Magnus doubt it? He scanned the bloodbath for somewhere to go, but there was nowhere.

Well, so what? Only cowards hid. Magnus knew he could not fight this battle; it would be for him a mortal sin. So, with his heart racing wildly, yet strangely steeped in peace, he tossed aside his sword and reached instinctively for his crucifix. It was then that he remembered he did not have it. Aerling had never given it back in the cargo-hold, nor had Magnus asked for its return. His brother still had it with him, wherever he was, and that thought was most consoling.

Instead, Magnus pulled out his only other possession, his little worn prayerbook of psalms. Prayer would be both his weapon and his shield. What more did he need? He bent to his knees on the blood-splattered deck, and was instantly dumbfounded. He felt no pain. None at all.

Thus, with perfect trust in God's loving care, Magnus began to pray the psalms amidst the raging battle.

Chapter Twenty

It didn't take long for Kol to assess the damage once the Welsh ships had pulled back. It was the job of his father, Kali Saebjornson, to report to the king, but he'd been grievously wounded during the battle, so Kol took the duty upon himself. Berrfott would be impatient for news, and it was never wise to keep him waiting. With a last survey of the wreckage around him, Kol wiped the streaming sweat from his face and entered through the king's cabin door.

Berrfott was seated at table, his clothes just as bloodied as Kol's, but his servants had already brought him refreshments. At Kol's entrance he lowered the cup of mead in his hand, obviously surprised.

"Kol," he greeted. "I expected your father Kali."

"He is injured, Sire."

"Oh. I hadn't heard. Is it serious?"

"Yes, Sire. He is resting. I thought I would bring you word. The remainder of the Welsh fleet has finally turned back. Victory is ours."

The young king beamed. "Excellent!" He indicated towards the keg, inviting Kol to help himself. "What casualties? Are there many?"

"Fewer, Sire, than we would have dared hope," Kol answered, gratefully filling a cup for himself. "Only a handful of our nobles are dead, although several others are badly wounded. It could go either way with them." As he said it, he felt his heart clench at the thought of his father. *Please God,* he silently prayed, *do not let him die.*

"How fared the commoners?" the king wanted to know.

"We've lost a lot. The Welsh put up a good fight. It'll take some time to count."

The king nodded thoughtfully. "Well, it's unfortunate, but these things happen. The commoners are expendable at least. It's my nobles who concern me most."

Kol knew why. He thought, *And what will I receive if my father dies due to your stupidity?*

Those two Orkney princes had been right --- entering the Menai Strait was an idiotic move in the first place and had wasted too many lives. Kol's father was one of the most powerful and respected noblemen in Norway; if he should die because of this battle, the king by custom must compensate his son. Kol knew the payment could be monetary, or it might be made in the form of a gift. A larger estate perhaps, or a valuable team of horses . . . or even a wife. But Kol was not interested in Berrfott's gifts. He much preferred his father to recover and live.

The king, however, intent only upon his own problems, continued his inquiries. "The Orkney hostages I sent you to unchain," he asked, "what of them?"

"Oh, those two." With an effort Kol pulled his anxious thoughts away from his dying father. "The older one," he answered, "the one with the mouth, lies dead. Stabbed in the back by one of our crew, who didn't realize you had set him free on purpose. Stupid man thought he was trying to escape."

"Hmm, that would be Aerling, the Orkney crown-prince. Pity. He was most valuable."

"Valuable perhaps, but also extremely dangerous. You

should've seen him fight back in the Orkneys." Kol had. Thankfully from a distance. "He was taking out our men three at a time. Truly, Sire, I'm not exaggerating."

The king cocked an eyebrow. "That good?"

"He put our warriors to shame. I, for one, am relieved he's dead. He would have been a lion in captivity. I didn't trust him one bit."

A chuckle escaped the young monarch. "So, made of the same foul stuff as his cousin Hakon, was he?"

"Not at all," Kol defended him, despite himself. "Hakon Paalson is a traitor and a coward. The whole world can see that. Not so the sons of Erlend. They were bred of much sterner stuff, those two." Less than five minutes was all it had taken for Kol to sum them up. Unlike Hakon, they were both princes to the core.

"Well," the king decided, "in any case the younger one just doubled in ransom. He's the new heir to the Orkneys. If they want him back, they must pay accordingly. But tell me, Kalison, did either of them slay any of our crew?"

"No, Sire. They did not."

"Are you sure?"

"Positive."

"Then I shall be true to my word of honor and let their father live." He raised his drink in a mock toast. "Jarl Erlend shall enjoy all the luxuries my dungeon back home has to offer. Compliments of his two gallant sons." He drained the cup. "But you haven't told me, Kol, what happened to the tame one. Obviously he survived."

"Oh yes, he survived alright. But only Heaven knows how."

"Why? What happened to him?"

"Nothing, Sire. That's just it."

"What do you mean, nothing?"

Kol explained. "The lad refused to fight. He threw aside his sword and took out some little prayerbook he had on his person. Then he knelt down on the deck and simply started to pray."

He could see the king was skeptical, and small wonder. Kol would never believe it either, if he had not seen it with his own two eyes. Even the fact that Magnus could kneel at all was incredible. Kol knew he had not been faking down in the cargo-hold; he had been in genuine pain. Yet on the deck he had knelt on that mangled knee without the slightest sign of discomfort. How?

"Are you saying he did nothing but *pray* in the midst of fierce battle? Come now, Kalison. Surely you jest. He must've at least used a shield to ward off the blows of others."

"No, Sire. He had neither sword nor shield. I witnessed this myself. Men were being slaughtered all around him, yet he just knelt there in the thickening pool of blood, as if he didn't even notice, and chanted the psalms as peacefully as any monk in a chapel. Not one weapon struck him. He was completely unharmed."

Berrfott was frowning. "Impossible. If what you claim is true, he should be dead."

"I know, Sire. But he's not. If you ask me, God protected him miraculously. There's no other explanation."

"Don't make me laugh, Kalison. I would not have picked you as one to believe in such nonsense as miracles."

"Actually, Sire," Kol said without wavering, "I do. God never forsakes those who put their trust in Him. Obviously this young prince has unshakable confidence in our Heavenly Father."

He noticed the amusement in the king's eyes, but didn't care. At last Berrfott said, "I admit this is all most intriguing. I should like to make the acquaintance of one so extraordinarily favored by the gods."

"You mean the one true God," Kol corrected with a boldness somewhat uncharacteristic of him.

The king let it go. After all, Kol was the son of one of his most powerful warriors. All he said was, "Clean the boy up and treat those wounds of his properly. Are you capable of that, Kalison?"

"Yes, Sire. I can take care of him."

"Good. Do it. Then bring him to me."

Kol hesitated. He knew he was speaking out of place, but he said, "Sire, do not punish him for having not fought. He is an honorable lad and brave."

"I will not hurt him, if that is what you mean."

Kol wondered what Berrfott actually had in mind, but he bowed his head in submission and started to depart.

The king called him back. "Kalison, wait."

Kol stopped and turned back around. "Yes?"

"What was his name again? I confess I've forgotten."

"His name, Sire, is Magnus."

"How marvelously appropriate. Latin for great." Berrfott chuckled. "Maybe we should call him Magnus-the-Great. Or else, Magnus-the-Great-Coward, for not wanting to fight. What do you think, my good Kol?"

"Actually, after what I witnessed this day, I'm somewhat inclined to call him Magnus-the-Saint." It was only half a jest.

Now the king laughed outright. "Call him whatever strikes your fancy. I really don't care. Just fix him up and bring him into my royal presence."

Chapter Twenty-One

The last thing in the world Magnus desired was to come face to face with that odious Viking sea-wolf. Treatment for his wounds he accepted gratefully, but as for the meal brought to him afterwards, Magnus couldn't bring himself to touch it. His brother was dead. The thought of food only made him feel sick.

To his surprise, the Norwegian seemed to understand. In fact, Magnus could not help notice that he actually looked sad himself. "Will you at least eat a little?" he asked, not unkindly. "You're half starved. You need something to strengthen you."

Magnus looked at him, wondering if this man were friend or foe. He tried to remember his name from earlier in the cargo-hold. Kol. Yes, that was it. Kol Kalison. The Norseman had treated him with surprising mercy, even respect, ever since the battle a few hours ago, but Magnus couldn't figure out why. After all, Kol had seen him throw aside his sword and refuse to fight for Berrfott as ordered. If anything, he should be dealing with Magnus contemptuously. But he wasn't. Just the opposite.

Kol said, "Take at least a few bites, Prince Magnus. You really must." He hesitated, then added, "I know just how you feel. You lost your brother. My father died too, hardly half an hour ago."

His words were unexpected. No wonder he looked as if a sword had just passed through his heart. Magnus felt a stab of genuine sorrow for this stranger's grief. "I'm very sorry," he said.

"I didn't know."

"I would never have expected you to. Now eat. The king wants to see you, and patience is not one of his shining qualities. The longer it takes me to bring you to him, the more we'll both suffer for it."

They were enemies of course, himself and Kol Kalison. But they were both children of God. Where other Vikings still wore the pagan hammer of Thor, Magnus noticed that Kol wore a crucifix without shame. It wasn't his fault that he had been born in Norway, nor that his monarch had decided unjustly to invade the Orkneys, anymore than it was Magnus's fault that his own cousin Hakon had brought such appalling suffering and devastation into so many innocent lives.

Hakon. His very own kith and kin. If it had not been for his treachery, neither Magnus nor Kol Kalison would be here in the first place. None of this would have happened. Magnus would not be hostage upon an enemy warship, alone and wounded, somewhere off the coastline of Wales. No, he would be peacefully in the Orkneys, living his normal life, with his father securely upon the throne.

And Aerling. Aerling would be alive.

An almost suffocating sorrow gripped him. He had to remind himself of his own words, practically the last he had ever spoken to his brother . . . *We will each die when we are meant to, Aerling, in exactly the way God has ordained from eternity. There is nothing we can do to add one day, nor even one single moment, to the time allotted us by our Creator.* Magnus had believed those words when he had said them, when they both thought that he, not Aerling, would be the one to get killed. He must likewise believe them now. It was not Hakon's betrayal which had ended his brother's life so young and so tragically. No, it was God's holy and adorable Will, and had been decreed even before the creation of time, as had everyone's moment and manner of death. Magnus knew he must cling to that thought, lest, after having suffered so much to win for Aerling the grace of conversion, he himself fall prey to the same trap of Satan and end up despising their cousin in his own heart. He realized now just how easy it would be to hate Hakon for his brother's death. He must fight the temptation before Lucifer got away with it.

"Are you alright?" Kol was looking at him with concern.

"No," Magnus answered with honesty. But neither was Kol, for that matter. The sense of loss was crushing, for both of them.

There was something in the Norwegian's eyes which said he understood perfectly. He too had just been asked by God to accept a very heavy cross. It was an odd feeling, but somehow Magnus sensed that, given a different time and other circumstances, he and Kol Kalison could have easily become friends. He suspected it was mutual.

"What was your father's name?"

"Kali Saebjornson. Why do you ask?"

"Just so that I can pray for him. That's all."

Kol was taken aback. "Thank you," he said. "That's very kind of you." Then he added, "I'll pray for your brother too." Magnus could tell he meant it, even though it had been very obvious that he had not liked Aerling at all in their one brief meeting of this morning.

Was it truly only this morning, a mere few hours ago, that Kol had come down to unchain them? It seemed to Magnus a whole other lifetime that he and Aerling had been having such fun ridiculing these Norsemen, all of which had been said at Kol's expense. Well, Kol obviously didn't hold it against him.

"I'm sure my brother will be very grateful for your prayers,"

Magnus told him. "He might need a few." He felt certain that Aerling had saved his soul, an eleventh-hour worker, but there was still Purgatory . . . which very few escaped entirely, even amongst the best of God's friends.

He could not help it; the horrifying image came back of his brother's dead body before the crew had dumped it over the side of the ship into the cold, black waters of the sea. They had shown Magnus on purpose, of course --- had carried the corpse over to him after the battle, so that he could see with his own eyes the agonizing death Aerling must have died, with that sword still impaled straight through his spine. Then one of the Norwegians had yanked it out in front of him, its crimson blade dripping with blood, and before Magnus could even react, the men had laughed and heaved the body overboard. The memory would haunt him for life.

He must not let himself hate Hakon! *Go away, Lucifer!* he thought, *I will not give in!*

Still, despite everything, Kol was right. Magnus must eat at least a little of the food in front of him. He had no idea what Berrfott was going to do to him; for all he knew the starvation torture might begin all over again. He was already much too weakened by all that had passed and he must try to regain his strength. For like it or not, Magnus was the Orkney crown-prince now, and as of this day the responsibility of his father's kingdom lay on his shoulders. He must attempt an escape if ever he could, just as Aerling had been obliged to try when he was the heir.

So, for his desolate people back home, and for them alone, Jarl Erlend's surviving son forced himself to eat.

Chapter Twenty-Two

Kol was surprised with himself, and even a little ashamed of his sentiments, as he stood at the prisoner's side in the presence of his king. It seemed disloyal of him, to say the least, to feel more natural affinity with this young enemy prince, whom he had known hardly more than a few hours, than with his own liege-lord, to whose service he had pledged himself and to whom he owed every obedience. But there it was and it could not be helped. Of the two royal personages with him in this ship's small cabin, Kol Kalison knew exactly which one he liked and which one he did not. He decided he had better keep his mouth shut and not say a thing.

He, together with Magnus, had been standing here in front of the seated king for what seemed an awfully long time, whilst Berrfott silently sized up his hostage. He was in no hurry; he could drag this out as long as he wished and no one could do a thing about it. Kol found it unnecessarily mean that he did not at least allow the prisoner to sit down. Berrfott knew full well that Magnus was wounded, and were it not for Kol's help, would hardly be able to stand at all. At least not for this long. But the king was doing it on purpose. No doubt waiting for Magnus to ask him for mercy.

But it was obvious, even to Kol, that the Orkney prince would not give him that satisfaction. Magnus would grit his teeth and bear the pain till the end of the world before he would beg a thing from Norway. Even a chair. And yes, anyone could see that he was

135

equally sizing up his captor.

The frigid silence was starting to drag just a bit too long for comfort and Kol was wondering if he should venture to break it. But thankfully he did not have to, for at that moment, Magnus had also had enough.

"What did you summon me here for?" he demanded. No 'your Majesty' or anything. For the way he said it, he could have been the one sitting on the throne.

Berrfott's eyes were ice, but he settled himself back and managed to conjure up some sort of a smile, which didn't fool anyone. He decided at last to motion towards a chair. "I can see you are in a lot of pain, my friend. Do sit."

Magnus stayed exactly where he was.

"I insist," the king said.

The prince did not move.

"Sit!" Berrfott thundered. It was a command this time; no mistake about it.

The Orkney heir remained standing in precisely the same spot. Kol could see their eyes lock in silent warfare. He had to resist the urge to give Magnus a stern nudge in the back as a warning to obey. After all, Kol Kalison knew this monarch. Poor Magnus Erlendson did not. Kol feared the boy was going to be learning the hard way.

Unexpectedly, it was Berrfott himself who broke the deadlock. He started to chuckle, as if he found his prisoner's defiance suddenly funny. Then he turned to Kol and chided, "And you led me to believe this was the submissive one. You were mistaken, Kalison. The younger brother is streaked with exactly the same insolence as the older one was. There is no difference between them whatsoever."

"Why did you bring me here?" Magnus demanded again.

"What do you want from me?"

"Want from you? Ah, my poor friend, you misunderstand my intentions. I want nothing from you. It is I who desire to give."

"I will accept no bribes from Norway."

"Now, now. I wish only to offer you my sincere condolences regarding the death of your brother. I grieve with you deeply."

"I have no doubt that you do."

Kol knew exactly what Magnus meant by that. Aerling's ransom would have been staggering. Poor Berrfott. All that potential gold, just dumped over the ship into the sea.

The king said, "His death was a most unfortunate accident."

"An accident. Oh, I see. Just like all my butchered countrymen back in the Orkneys? Are those your little accidents too?"

Kol thought of his own father, lifeless and pale and wrapped in a winding sheet, and wondered if King Berrfott would brush him aside as a mere mishap as well. The Battle of Menai Strait could have easily been avoided. It was the foolishness alone of the greedy monarch which had caused untold losses of life, and Kol knew in his heart the skirmish had been unjust before God.

Berrfott said, "You refused to fight. Why?"

"My father and my uncle had a truce with the Welsh. I did nothing more than honor it. To act otherwise would have been to violate my conscience."

The king looked amused. "Your conscience. Hah! Another one of these sanctimonious Christians who live their creed, are you? I've discovered there's a few of those around here."

Kol suspected the jab was intended for himself as much as for Magnus. But he didn't care. Neither, obviously, did the Orkney prince, who would not deign to reply.

Berrfott continued. "Your brother was not the only one who

was killed this day. Regrettably, my faithful cup-bearer did not survive the battle either. His was a position of the highest honor, and I need a man to replace him. I should like to bestow that privilege upon you."

Kol could hardly believe his ears. For one of common blood it was, yes, an immense honor to bear the vessel of a king. But for a prince, and one held hostage at that, the mere suggestion was an affront and a mockery.

If Kol was shocked, Magnus was more so, and rightly. He said angrily, "I am a prince."

"You are a *slave*."

"Then lock me straight back in chains and throw me below deck! I will *never* serve wine to the man who stole my father's throne and spilled the blood of my brother."

Seemingly out of the wild blue, Berrfott calmly said, "Your sister Gunnhild. She is beautiful." He smiled. "In fact, she is simply stunning."

Magnus instantly froze. Even Kol was taken aback. Berrfott let the subtle suggestion sink in, good and deep, then continued, "Perhaps as her younger brother you never took notice of these things. But most men can only dream of a woman like her." He looked at Kol and winked. "I am sure Kalison here agrees."

Kol could neither agree nor disagree. He had never seen the girl in his life. But what he did see was the fear that leapt instantly into Magnus's eyes. His expression seemed to say to Berrfott, *Don't you dare.*

"But I have no need to stop at dreams, do I? For I am now gentle Gunnhild's lord and master. I have the power to do with your sister whatever I choose. She is my subject and I am her king. Stop and think about that, Erlendson."

Instinctively, probably without even realizing it, Magnus

turned to Kol, as if urgently begging for help.

"Don't worry; she's not on this ship." The words were out before Kol could stop them. It was small reassurance, but he saw Magnus relax a little. Kol knew this was probably nothing more than a scare-tactic. There was no possible way that Berrfott could have laid eyes on either one of Jarl Erlend's daughters, anymore than Kol himself had. They had not been taken captive. They were both still in the Orkneys, and any knowledge of Princess Gunnhild or her pretty looks would have come solely from her cousin Hakon Paalson. But Magnus, of course, had no way of knowing that.

Almost casually, the king returned to their earlier conversation. "So, my slave refuses to serve my wine, does he?"

The cruel blackmail had the effect Berrfott hoped for. Kol heard Magnus let out an almost imperceptible moan and he suddenly looked even wearier and more vulnerable than he had in the cargo-hold. Which was saying a lot. There was no need to reply. Both Norwegians knew he would submit now to anything.

"Kalison, take him away. I have other things now to deal with. Unless, of course, my new servant has anything to say?"

"No," Magnus answered with disgust. "I have nothing to say to you. And never shall."

Berrfott laughed, then added for him, "Your Majesty."

The cup-bearer had no choice. "Your Majesty," he repeated.

"You learn very quickly, Erlendson. Lucky for you."

But Kol could see, even if the king could not, that despite all the humiliation and pain he had been through, there was still plenty of fire left in the young prince's eyes.

"Kalison, show him where the wine is kept."

"Yes, Sire." Kol dutifully bowed his head in token respect, and, moving closer, gave Magnus his shoulder to lean on.

As the two of them departed, Kol could not help wonder if

Berrfott really would do anything to Magnus's sister. He was inclined to doubt it.

But he was wrong. Completely wrong.

The king of Norway was already making plans for the lovely Orkney princess. Plans which the son of the late Kali Saebjornson would indeed find out in the not too distant future.

Magnus, however, would not learn of his sister's fate for many long years to come.

Chapter Twenty-Three

The following weeks as the king's cup-bearer were amongst the most miserable of Magnus's life. The feeling of sadness over Aerling's death, together with the loneliness which faced him now, was close to overwhelming. In a certain sense, the new ordeal was almost worse than the last. He missed his brother so much. And the responsibility he now felt as his father's heir was staggering.

A few of the Norwegians on the boat were highly amused by his situation and treated him with calculated cruelty. Apart from those, most of the crew simply ignored him, for which he was relieved. He wanted no part with them and was only too happy to stay to himself. The only one who showed him genuine kindness was Kol, yet Magnus was starting to find that that actually made things harder. He felt such a strong natural friendship between them that he had to continually be on his guard, afraid that he might accidentally confide too much to the sympathetic young nobleman, who was, after all, still the enemy. Thus Magnus carefully avoided Kol's company whenever he could, which for some reason added greatly to his feeling of loneliness.

Day after day as he carried that loathsome cup filled with the king's wine, he thought of almost nothing but escape. His knee was ever so slowly healing, as were his other wounds. At least he could walk unaided now, and, given a few more weeks and the right chance, he might eventually be able to make a run for it.

Berrfott's fleet was raiding and plundering every coastline, and often they were anchored near land. But to his frustration, there was never a moment when he was not watched, except when the ship was far out at sea. Thus the long and lonely weeks dragged. It was starting to seem as if the chance to bolt was never going to arrive.

And then came the night of the storm.

* * * * * *

"What?" roared the king. "What is this you're saying?" He looked around at the faces in his cabin. Vidkunn, Serk, Skopti and Ogmund. Trusted nobles, every one. The only notable warrior absent was Kalison. "Are you telling me that my cup-bearer has escaped?"

"It seems so, Sire," Serk answered. "He's nowhere to be found. The entire ship has been searched."

"Impossible!" Berrfott bellowed. "He must be on board! Where could he possibly have gone?"

It was Vidkunn who answered. "The only thing we can think of is those few hours last night during the storm. The winds blew us way off course and for awhile we weren't far from the coast of Scotland. I know this sounds improbable, Sire, but maybe he slipped overboard and tried to swim to land."

"Surely not, Vidkunn. He would've had to be insane! That squall was vicious. No one could swim through that." Berrfott shook his head. "His leg wasn't even healed yet."

Skopti said, "I agree. That water would've been freezing. I don't think he tried."

"Neither do I," Berrfott said. "Search the ship again."

"Sire, I'm telling you," Vidkunn insisted, "our men have

looked everywhere. There is nowhere for him to hide. He had to have jumped. It's the only explanation."

"Of course he jumped," Serk cut in. "The cook told me that his bed was arranged this morning to look as if he was still in it. He piled the blankets in such a way that it took the cook a few minutes to realize it was actually empty."

"Which means the escape was planned all along," Vidkunn concluded.

Berrfott was furious. "Then put out the order to turn this vessel around," he snapped. "We are heading straight back to Scotland. Immediately."

The men exchanged doubtful glances, then someone asked, "Sire, are you serious?"

"Of course I'm serious! Have you forgotten that we are speaking about the heir to the Orkney throne? I lost his brother's ransom; I'm not going to let this one get away."

"If he jumped last night," Ogmund said, "he is most certainly dead. And if he isn't, he could be anywhere out there, Sire. We'll be searching for weeks."

"No we won't," the king assured. "We have hunting dogs on this ship, do we not? Uncage them and find something the boy left behind. The hounds will pick up his scent. If Erlend's son is alive, we are going to find him."

Chapter Twenty-Four

Magnus had no idea in the world how he'd made it this far, but he had . . . and he was free. He didn't even know what country this was, which made him feel vulnerable, but it wasn't Norway, of that he was sure, and that's all that mattered.

A terrible storm during the night had tossed the ship every which way and he had glimpsed a chunk of land out there. He could never have attempted an escape with Aerling in the Menai Strait; it would have been for him suicidal. But his knee wasn't as bad now as it had been back then, and it hadn't seemed unreasonable last night to try.

Or so he had thought at the time.

That was before he had realized how cold that water was going to be and how long he would be in the sea. It had taken him a couple hours to fight his way through the churning black waves, the last half of which had become a living nightmare. So many times he was sure he would drown. Then somehow, right when he knew he could not possibly go on, he hit shallow water. He had miraculously made it onto the beach, then simply collapsed.

That was the last thing he could remember.

Now the blinding morning sun was shining in his face and Magnus groggily awoke from his exhausted sleep. It took him a long moment to even realize where he was. He felt so sick. He sat up in the sand, shivering, as spasms of cold coursed through him. His clothes were clinging to him, soaking wet. He was freezing and feverish and noticed with dismay that the wound on his knee had partially reopened. It felt so bad that he didn't want to move. But he knew he was going to have to.

He looked around. The beach was totally deserted, the forest beyond it wild. Where was this? Was there a village nearby, or a farm, or even a shepherd's hut? Was there another human being anywhere within miles that he could reach for help? It certainly didn't look like it. This seemed like the untamed back of nowhere. Magnus suspected he was in trouble. Big trouble. Now what?

A little afraid and very shaky, Magnus made it to his feet. Pain bolted through his leg, just like it had weeks ago. He tried to ignore it and decide what to do. The most urgent thing for survival right now was probably a fire to dry his clothes and warm himself. And then he needed water. Those two things. Everything else was secondary and could wait. But fire and water, he feared, could prove very difficult to find.

He limped a little way into the forest. Find wood. Twigs, branches, anything that might burn. He needed to build a fire urgently. He knew that even if he gathered enough wood, he had no flint with which to light it. No weapon if he required one, no food . . . and no drinkable water. Maybe he should instead look for that first, because, frankly, he was feeling so weak he thought he might faint.

Sitting quickly on the ground, he prayed the dizziness would pass. If he blacked out now, who was to say he would ever get up again. He knew he was burning high with fever, no doubt from being so long in the freezing cold sea, and he felt strangely disoriented. But God had gotten him this far; surely He would not abandon him now.

How long Magnus sat there with the trees spinning crazily around him he had no idea. *Please, Lord,* he begged, *help me.*

Eventually the woods stopped rotating and settled back down. He thought, *Find water. Look for a stream.* He struggled painfully to his feet for the second time. Then something, or someone --- his angel perhaps --- made him look back around towards the beach.

That's when he saw it.

The warship. It was coming back! Coming back to find him!

Something like panic seized him. He had to get out of here! Adrenalin came to the rescue and gave him the almost superhuman strength he needed to move. He stumbled farther into the dense woods, frantically looking for a place to hide. Running was impossible; the best he could do was limp, and even that was difficult enough.

Blessed Virgin, he implored, *Saint Joseph! Help me get away! Saint Olaf the Viking, please don't let them find me!* Yes, even the enemy Norsemen could claim at least one canonized saint, and he had been king of Norway at that! Magnus felt sure that the holy Olaf Haraldson was listening from Heaven.

He must have been, for the impossible was happening. Despite his fever and shivering and the terrible pain in his leg, Magnus was actually making it deeper into the forest. The boat had not yet even anchored. Maybe the crew had not seen him. He slowed down, thinking that perhaps he was safe after all.

And then he heard the dogs.

Chapter Twenty-Five

The king's men were baffled. The hounds had the scent alright. They were going wild, the whole pack of them, right below this one tree. They were yelping and leaping and falling all over each other as if they were crazed with excitement.

But the tree was empty.

"I don't understand this," Vidkunn said. "It makes absolutely no sense. This pack is never wrong." He looked at Skopti beside him, confused. Everyone knew these dogs were the best hunters in Norway. They didn't make mistakes like this. Certainly not all of them at once. So where was the boy?

Equally perplexed, Skopti only shrugged. It was Ogmund behind them who spoke. "He's simply not up there. It's obvious."

"If he was hiding anywhere in those branches," Vidkunn agreed, "we would see him. There is no way in the world we could miss a person up there."

"Let's go. We're wasting our time."

"The king will kill us."

"Then what do you suggest? Any ideas?"

The warriors looked at each other helplessly. Finally Vidkunn said, "Alright. Let's find the nearest village. Ask around a bit. Maybe someone has seen him. He'll be pretty recognizable, especially with wet clothes and his leg still bandaged."

Skopti said, "Sounds good to me. Let's scout around for a

couple hours. I don't know about the rest of you, but I certainly don't want to admit to the king we lost him."

"You can say that again. I enjoy living."

"We all do, Serk ."

"Let's go."

Vidkunn called the hounds and the men wandered off as Magnus watched in stunned silence. He was right there, hardly twenty feet above them, plain as day in the straggly branches of the tree. He was stupefied. Then again, maybe he shouldn't be. Had not God protected him by supernatural means in the past?

Thank you, Saint Olaf, he thought in his heart. The canonized Norwegian king had called off his men from Heaven.

But now that the miraculous episode was past, Magnus found himself left again to his own human resources. The waves of dizziness came back with a vengeance and for a moment he wondered how he was ever going to climb back down out of this tree.

But he didn't need to. He was about to descend the fast way. For at that instant his vision started to blur and Magnus realized he was blacking out.

He tried desperately to keep his hold but was unable. Suddenly he was falling, crashing through the tangle of rough branches towards the ground twenty feet below. He landed with a thud that seemed to shatter his whole body. There was a moment of blinding pain, then came that darkness, welcome and merciful, which took all feeling away.

Chapter Twenty-Six

There were sounds, low and gentle, floating around him, but hard as he tried Magnus could not quite hold on to them. He had the impression they might be voices, female voices, but he was not sure at all if they were.

He was hot. Burning in fact, yet shivering at the same time. There was a sensation of something cool being pressed against his forehead, taking away some of the heat, and that kindly voice, if it were a voice, was speaking to him again. Yet he couldn't make out any words.

Where am I? he wondered vaguely, but was in too much pain to really care. He felt like his body had been smashed to pieces. He tried to remember what had happened to him, but there were only disjointed snatches of memory . . . A tree, dogs barking, something about Saint Olaf. None of it seemed to make any sense.

The blackness was starting to return. He wanted to succumb to it. Unconsciousness was blessedness . . . it made the pain go away. He didn't want to wake up, but in some region of his mind he understood that darkness such as this was dangerous. It could make a man die. He must try to pull out of it. *Wake up,* he ordered himself. *Open your eyes.*

". . . coming to. Mairee, fetch some broth . . ."

The fragmented sentence flitted past and was gone.

His eyelids felt like lead. Somehow he forced them open. At first all he could see was blurry shapes, but gradually they resolved themselves into objects and his surroundings came into some kind of focus. This was a room, which surprised him. He had never seen this place before. Beautiful rich tapestries hung from the walls, their bright woven colors almost startling against the drab stone. A fire crackled on a hearth nearby. A lady was standing next to the bed, looking down at him.

She smiled reassuringly. "Don't be afraid," she told him. "You're safe. You're with friends." Her eyes were unlike any he had ever seen before. They were gentleness itself.

A younger female appeared beside her, wearing an apron and holding a steaming bowl in her hands. She had rosy cheeks with freckles, and could not have been too much younger than he was. With a somewhat nervous giggle, she offered him the bowl.

Well, he was obviously expected to sit up and take it. This might not be so easy. He could hardly move for all the pain. But somehow he managed to sit up enough to accept the drink.

"Thank you," he said, feeling ever so groggy.

The girl gave him a shy little curtsey, tried hard not to giggle again, and stepped behind her mistress, blushing.

The older lady must have been in her forties, but even so her beauty and graceful bearing could not fail to be noticed. Magnus had never seen such pure and kind eyes. "My name is Margaret," she introduced herself. "And this is Mairee, one of my maidens-in-waiting."

So, Magnus thought, *nobility.*

His head was spinning. He felt so sick. All he wanted was to lie back down. But that would be rude, so he forced himself not to. "Where am I?" he asked.

"You are in Scotland. This is my husband's castle."

This was a castle? He didn't remember anything about a castle. How did he get here in the first place?

Seeing his confusion, the lady explained. "Some hunters found you lying unconscious in the woods. That was nearly two days ago. At first they thought you were dead, but when they saw you were alive, they brought you here to me. Now drink. The broth will give you strength."

He had been unconscious *two days?* No wonder he felt the way he did. He obeyed and took a few sips of the hot broth. It made him feel a little better.

The Lady Margaret went on, "God is most merciful. Had you not been discovered when you were, I fear you would not have lived much longer. You were soaking wet and all but frozen. Not even to mention your injuries! What happened to you out there?"

"I . . . can't remember."

"I'm not surprised. You've been delirious with fever. Whatever happened, you have obviously been through a lot. Drink a little more. Then you can lie down again."

He obeyed and had more of the broth. He wished his head would clear so he could think straight.

Lady Margaret said, "That wound on your knee didn't happen two days ago. You were hurt before this, weren't you? Something most terrible must have caused that."

For a moment, Magnus's mind remained blank. Then it came back. "The Norwegians," he said. "One of them tried to kill me with an axe. But . . . that was ages ago. Back home."

The young one, Mairee, cringed with horror. Magnus instantly regretted saying it. His own sisters, Gunnhild and Cecily, would have taken the gory statement with hardly a blink of an eye. But they were the daughters of a warlord and bloodshed for them was a normal part of life, just as it had always been for him and Aerling. Mairee obviously wasn't like that. In fact, he noticed now that she looked exceptionally innocent, as if she had been

151

sheltered from violence and couldn't bear the thought of anyone being hacked up with an axe blade. Magnus himself had never thought twice about it. Battle was battle, simple as that. But with the memory of Berrfott's invasion, all the other memories instantly flooded back. "I remember now," he said. "The dogs. They were after me. King Berrfott of Norway ---"

"Yes, that part we know," Lady Margaret gently interrupted. "Some of his men came to the village looking for you. They stayed many hours, searching the houses and asking questions. Our people were very frightened. But you are safe now, I promise. The Norwegian ship has departed. You are under my husband's protection." She turned to the other and said, "Mairee, bring him more to drink." Then to Magnus, "Do you want to try to eat something? Are you cold? I can get you more blankets."

She reminded him of his mother back home.

"I'll be alright. Thank you."

"Are you going to tell us," she asked with a teasing smile, "who you are? Or are we meant to spend the next few days guessing? You do, uh, have a name, don't you?"

"You mean, the Norwegians didn't tell you who I am?"

The lady looked surprised. "No. Should have they?"

Now Magnus hesitated. They didn't know who he *was?* It had been rude, he suddenly realized, not to have introduced himself earlier, and it was going to be ruder by far not to do so now. But he was worth a sizable ransom, and it might not be a smart move to go blurting his identity to just anyone. He certainly had no desire to be held hostage again. He must find out whom this lady's husband was before saying too much. He knew instinctively that he could trust Lady Margaret and her innocent maiden-in-waiting. But the noblewoman's spouse might be a different story.

"Forgive me, my lady," he said. "Will you be so gracious as to tell me first in whose castle I find myself?"

He could see by her eyes that she immediately understood the question. This lady was anything but stupid. She knew now that whoever he was, he was valuable.

Her answer came with a little smile, as if it were a playful challenge. "You find yourself, young sir, in the castle of His Majesty King Malcolm Canmore."

Whoa! He reeled. This was the residence of the king of Scotland! He could not have landed in a higher spot if he'd tried.

Two thoughts immediately raced each other across his mind. The first was that his grandmother Ingibjorg, after having been widowed by Thorfinn the Mighty, had remarried. Her new husband had been none other than the same Malcolm Canmore, making him, at least temporarily, the stepfather of both Orkney Jarls. Queen Ingibjorg had died many years ago, even before Magnus had been born, but that relationship alone would surely make the Scottish king partial to him.

The second thought, following swiftly upon the first, assured him even further that he was in safe hands. For if this lady to whom he was speaking was the king's present wife, she could only be one person . . . Queen Margaret the Saint! Magnus had heard so much about her. Everyone had! She was a living legend, one of the holiest women alive. As the realization hit him, Magnus found himself suddenly awed. Imagine . . . being in the presence of an actual *saint,* one who would doubtless be someday canonized! Oh yes, he could trust her! He knew now he was in no danger in this castle, nor in this foreign land.

"I am," he instantly admitted, "the heir to the Orkney throne."

Across the room, poor little Mairee looked like she was going to fall over. She nearly dropped the soup. She'd already been watching him closely enough with huge love-struck eyes; it was impossible for him not to notice. Now she was *really* impressed.

The queen was taken aback, but only for an instant. Then she nodded, as if she was not all that surprised by his identity. She said, "I should've known. The Norwegians were far too anxious to find you. They even threatened the villagers with violence, hoping to force them to speak. But no one could give any information. The hunters had not yet found you. See how God works everything out for the good?"

"I'm so sorry, my lady, if I endangered your people. Forgive me."

"There's nothing to forgive you for. I'm only too happy you are alive and safe." Then she smiled that kind smile and added, "I've heard so many wonderful things about your grandmother Ingibjorg from my husband. I know he loved her dearly. You are most welcome here, Prince Aerling. You shall be our honored guest."

Her mistake, although unintentional, was like a sudden knifethrust in his heart. "I . . . am his younger brother," he faltered. "Aerling is . . . he died. My name is Magnus."

The queen looked appalled by her error. Then her expression gave way to genuine compassion. "Forgive me, my poor friend," she said. "I did not realize. I am so sorry."

"It's alright. There was no way you were to know." He hesitated, then added, "It was only recently."

"I'm so sorry," she repeated. "He will be in my prayers. I'm sure my chaplain will be only too happy to offer Masses for his soul if I ask him to."

Magnus thought, *How lucky could Aerling be? The intercession of a living saint!* He said, "Thank you, my lady. You don't know how grateful I am." Maybe the prayers of someone so holy would shorten his brother's time in Purgatory.

Mairee returned then with her soup, some sloshed over the side of the bowl where she had spilled it, looking even more shy --- if that were possible --- than she had before.

The queen said, "You must eat and rest as much as you can. It's going to take some weeks before you start feeling normal, I'm afraid."

"I don't have that time to spare, my lady. I need to get back to the Orkneys. My father and uncle, the two Jarls, are both in prison. I have to return and somehow help my people."

To his surprise, Lady Margaret firmly shook her head. "You are going nowhere, my brave young prince, in the condition you're in. Don't even think of it."

"But ---"

"The answer is absolutely no." Then she must have seen his dismay, for her tone softened and she explained, "You stand no chance, none at all, against this King Berrfott, unless you return to your kingdom with an army. Even my own husband, for all his power, has been forced in this last month to cede a large portion of his lands to Norway, in order to prevent war from falling upon our country. Please, Prince Magnus, listen to me. My husband will speak to you if you prefer, as also will any of our sons, but I know exactly what all of them will tell you. To show up in the Orkneys now will accomplish nothing, other than endangering your life."

Magnus wondered what Aerling would do, if he were the one here. Knowing him, he would take the risk, with or without an army. So then would Magnus. "I have to go back," he repeated. "Even if only to protect my mother and sisters." He thought of Berrfott's blackmail to him regarding Gunnhild. Whether it had been an empty threat or not, Magnus did not know. Kol obviously had thought it was nothing but a scare-tactic, but he could have been wrong.

To his surprise, Lady Margaret said, "If your mother and sisters are still there, it is all the more reason for you to stay away. Your return would put them in danger. Besides, as the heir, you owe it to your people to stay alive. In God's own good time, He may well return your kingdom to its rightful line, that of your grandfather Thorfinn. But only if such is for His glory. That is for Him to decide, not you."

Coming from one so close to God, how could Magnus argue?

"I fear then, my lady," he said, "that I am completely at the mercy of Scotland."

"We will be delighted, Prince Magnus, to have you stay. Our home is yours, until God shows you otherwise."

He was blessed, of course, to have such a protectress, and was grateful to Heaven for it. Yet little did Magnus know that within less than a year both Saint Margaret and King Malcolm would be dead, and that his sojourn in Scotland would be much longer than he could ever imagine.

Chapter Twenty-Seven

(Scotland, ten years later)

Magnus simply could not believe whom he found waiting for him in the guesthouse. He had been fetched by a servant with the announcement that two unknown travelers had arrived at the castle claiming they were looking for him. Who they were or why they had come, the servant could not say.

Now, as he stood here in the doorway before them, he was all but speechless.

"Tor! Holbodi!" he exclaimed, "Is it really you? I . . . can't believe this."

"Nor can we, Lord Magnus. It's been ten years." The Chieftains both came forward and warmly clasped hands with their young master. "Look at you," Holbodi said, "how much you've grown up."

"Imagine, hiding away in Scotland all this time! So close to home and we never even knew."

"I have not been hiding, Tor. I had nowhere else to go. I had to let the Norwegians believe I was dead."

"You had us believing it too, my lord."

"The Scots have been so good to me; I can't even begin to tell you. They could not have treated me better were I one of King Malcolm's own sons. And back when he was alive, and the saintly Queen Margaret, their kindness was simply unsurpassed. But don't just stand there, you two. Sit down, please."

The Chieftains waited until he did first, then pulled up chairs for themselves. "We come with much news, Lord Magnus."

"I'm sure you do. But please, tell me first, how is my mother? Is she well?"

Tor beamed. "She is doing excellently. She will be so very relieved to learn that you're alive. And her little son Karl, he's been so excited that we're looking for you. He can't wait to finally meet---" He stopped abruptly at the look on Magnus's face and his sentence trailed off.

"Her . . . little *son?*" Magnus repeated blankly.

There was an awkward silence.

Then Holbodi said, "Oh dear."

"What are you talking about? My father was never released from Norway."

Tor looked anything but comfortable. He cleared his throat. "Um . . . have you . . . have you not heard, my lord?"

"No. I've heard nothing."

The Chieftains looked horrified.

"Forgive us, my lord. We thought you knew."

"Knew what?" Was this good news or bad? Magnus had no idea what to expect. He looked searchingly from one face to the other.

Tor and Holbodi exchanged a helpless glance. It was obvious that neither wanted to be the one to tell him and were both wildly hoping the other would volunteer.

Finally it was Holbodi, whom Magnus knew had been his father's closest friend, who broke it to him. "We are so sorry, my lord. Your father passed away in prison many years ago. He is buried in Trondheim."

"My father is . . . dead?"

"We're very sorry," Tor repeated. "I can't believe you didn't know. He died within less than two years of being taken captive. Your uncle Paal as well. It seems the Norwegians treated them most cruelly."

Magnus knew this would take awhile to sink in. In his heart he said a prayer for their souls, but felt numb with shock. The two Chieftains were silent now, obviously unwilling to go on with their news, as if they had badly messed up. Magnus didn't want them to feel bad; after all, they had done nothing wrong in telling him. So, forcing a brave smile to cover up his own sorrow, he returned to what they had earlier been saying and asked, "So, what was this about my mother? You were telling me about her, uh, little son."

Holbodi reluctantly said, "Yes, my lord. She remarried. A very pleasant man from Paplay by the name of Zieggert. He's only a simple farmer, it is true, but he cares for her and she is content."

"Well, I'm very happy for her then," Magnus said, trying to feel it.

A stepfather? And . . . a new *brother*? What was his name again? Magnus couldn't even remember what they had said.

Tor ventured, "Have you . . . um . . . heard anything about King Berrfott?" They both seemed scared now to shock him any further. They must have realized that not much news had reached him here in Scotland.

"The last I heard of Berrfott was that he was still trying to subdue the headstrong Irish." Magnus had to smile a little at that. "One virtue he must possess is perseverance."

Now Tor laughed. "Persistent or not, he'll never get Ireland now. They slew him at the battle of Ulster."

So, the king of Norway was dead too. This certainly was an awful lot of news. Magnus sat there, a bit stunned, trying to absorb it all.

"I suppose then," he said, "that this makes his son Prince

Sigurd the ruler of the Orkneys. He was eight when he was left there, so he must be, what? Seventeen or eighteen by now?" He drew in a breath, troubled by the thought. "This doesn't sound too encouraging."

"Actually, my lord, I'm happy to tell you that you are wrong. Sigurd is long gone."

Magnus's head was really starting to spin. "Gone? You mean, he left?"

Tor grinned. "Young Sigs had enough of our rough lands. Unlike his greedy father, he never wanted us anyhow." He chuckled and added, "We did our utmost, my lord, to cause him nothing but trouble. I promise."

Magnus laughed. "Like true Orkney sons. Well done."

"Yes, poor Sigurd was only too eager to shake our dust from his feet and scuttle back home to snowy Norway. Not a bad youngster, if the truth be known, but we're glad we've seen the last of him."

"I'm sure you are. But . . ." Magnus frowned. "I fear I am at a loss. If Berrfott was killed and Sigurd took a hike, and my own father and uncle are . . ." he paused. The word hurt. ". . . if they're both dead, then who sits now upon the Orkney throne?"

"Ah. That, my lord, is precisely what has brought us here to Scotland. You are your father's heir. The nobles beg you to return with us and take your rightful place at Jarl Hakon's side."

"Jarl *Hakon*? You mean, he's still alive? And back home?" Now his mind was really reeling from all these twists and turns.

"Oh yes, my lord," Holbodi said. "Your cousin is very much alive and very much home."

Tor explained, "Berrfott had hardly been dead ten minutes when Hakon came crawling out of a hole somewhere and swooped upon the Orkney throne like a vulture. I suppose it was to be expected. He appointed that unsightly kinsman of his as the kingdom's standard-bearer." He glanced at Holbodi for the name he was after.

"Ofeig," the other Chieftain supplied.

"So, he survived too." Magnus couldn't decide what to think. What should he think? He had no idea.

Tor tried to help him out. "In all fairness, my lord, we must admit that years of captivity under King Berrfott did Hakon some good. He was forced to finally grow up a little. He is still no angel, believe me, but he rules the kingdom better than one would have dared expect."

"I'm relieved then for our people." Magnus meant it. God was most good. He could use anything as a source of grace, and if Hakon had matured into a fair ruler, then nothing could have heartened his younger cousin more.

"But that is not the point, my Lord Magnus," Tor was saying. "Half the kingdom --- well, actually *all* by right, but putting that aside --- belongs to you. Your brother Aerling is dead; his inheritance has passed to you."

"Sail home with us," Holbodi urged, "and claim your throne."

This was all too sudden. Magnus could not take it in, more less think of a reply. And, if he were completely honest with himself, he had no desire whatsoever to reign over the Orkneys. All he had ever wanted was a life of obscurity and prayer, away from war and violence and worldly affairs. He had found that here in Scotland and was loathe to leave. His Chieftains were asking too much.

"Our kingdom," he answered, "is no longer under foreign rule. It has been returned to the hands in which it rightfully belongs, that of the line of my grandfather, Thorfinn the Mighty. That's all that matters. Hakon is descended from the same line as I am. If he's doing not a bad job, then the Orkneys have no need of me."

"You are wrong, my lord. Do not deceive yourself, please," Tor said. "The Isles need you greatly."

Magnus considered for a long while then finally said, "Don't you realize the impossibility of what you are proposing? Even should I agree to go back with you, which I am not at all inclined to do, then Hakon will surely oppose me. It will spark off civil war. The kingdom will be torn in half." It will be, he thought to himself, just as bad as it would have been with Aerling and Hakon together. It would never work. "I'm sorry," he said, "but I refuse. Leave Hakon in peace as your sole Jarl. It's better that way for our people."

"No, my lord. You do not understand."

"I understand enough. I don't want the Orkneys ripped to shreds. People will take sides. You know they will. You have my answer."

The two older men looked at each other, obviously not happy. Then Holbodi begged, "Hear us out, please, Lord Magnus. Jarl Hakon will not withstand you, we promise. He has his hands full warring with a couple of upstart Chieftains named Dufniall and Thorbjorn."

The latter was a name Magnus had never heard, but Dufniall he knew well. "You're not talking about Dungad's son, are you?" he asked, surprised.

"Him exactly."

Dungad had been Erlend and Paal's cousin. Despite himself, Magnus felt a stab of anger at the injustice. "He has no right to the throne. None whatsoever."

Tor smiled. "Jarl Hakon's sentiments precisely, my lord."

Well, that raised a bit of Magnus's old fighting blood. Dufniall, of all people! It made him nearly boil.

Holbodi continued. "Unfortunately, Dufniall has gained a lot of support from the Shetlands. In fact, he's succeeded in raising an army. I guess all those years of unrest under Norway made him ambitious. And, alas, brutal. Thorbjorn is not quite as powerful, but he's getting there."

"If anything," Tor promised, "Jarl Hakon will welcome your help with open arms. He can't fight these two alone."

Magnus felt torn. He found it difficult to believe that Hakon would want him. He himself, of course, had long ago forgiven his cousin for everything. But had Hakon forgiven him? Sadly, Magnus could not erase from his memory their own personal parting in the Assembly Hall all those years ago, and his cousin's vow to spill his blood. To return to the Orkneys and assert his claim to Aerling's throne would surely bring domestic strife upon his kingdom.

"No," he said again. "I will not come. Even Dufniall is not reason enough to risk civil war between Hakon and myself."

"You would not divide the islands but unify them," Holbodi insisted. "You must believe us. Jarl Hakon would much prefer to share the Orkneys with you than to lose them altogether."

Magnus frowned. "He told you that?"

"He knows we are searching for you."

They were side-stepping the question, but Tor quickly added, "If you are still worried, my lord, we will take you first to Norway. The three sons of Berrfott --- Sigurd, Olaf, and Eystein --- all back you in your claim."

Magnus was staggered. "*Norway backs me*? Are you serious?"

The two old warriors looked mighty pleased with themselves. They had been saving this of course as the ace up their sleeves.

"Yes. They do. Unlike their father, they are merciful and just, all three of them. And yet still as powerful as Hades. I doubt Jarl Hakon will want to cross swords with them."

"No, I don't imagine he will," Magnus agreed. "But how do

you know they back me?"

"Because," Tor answered with a hint of mischief, "we went to see them and simply asked."

"You went to Norway?"

"We did. In fact, that is how we found out where you are. We had never thought of looking for you in Scotland."

Now Magnus was really confused. "You're saying the Norwegians knew I was here all along? That makes no sense, Tor."

"Not all of them knew. Most were convinced you were dead, that you could never have survived such an escape. But your brother-in-law tipped us off to search for you in Scotland."

"What on earth are you talking about? Who's my brother-in-law?"

He could tell they were actually enjoying themselves, teasing him now about all these things he did not know. Tor tried to hide his mischievous smile but couldn't quite manage. "There was a Norwegian landholder," he explained, "who died at the battle of Menai Strait. He was powerful and respected, a nobleman of exceptional standing, and Berrfott felt obliged to give the man's son some compensation for his death. So the king gave him . . ." Tor paused for effect, ". . . a beautiful Orkney princess to be his bride. She just so happens to be your sister Gunnhild. She is very happily wed and lives with her husband, thus your brother-in-law, at his estates in Agder, Norway. When we went recently to pay her our respects, he said that he knew you and suggested we might find you in Scotland." Tor's smile broadened. "He was convinced you had survived your escape, after the way God had protected you during the battle of Menai."

"He was there? At Menai Strait?"

"Yes, my lord. In fact, he told us the whole story. Does the name Kol Kalison sound at all familiar?"

"Kol! Are you serious? Of course I remember him! You mean . . . he married my sister?" Magnus was stunned. Then all at once it struck him --- was *that* Berrfott's threatening plan of what he would do to Gunnhild? Marry her off to one of his nobles? If only Magnus had known. But, at the time, even Kol himself had obviously been ignorant of the king's intentions.

"Finally," Magnus said, "you tell me good news. I'm so happy for both of them. I have no doubt Kol will take excellent care of her."

"They're very much in love," Holbodi told him. "They have two children. A daughter, Ingirid, and a son about three years old named Rognavald." He too was smiling widely. "In looks, the little imp is identical to his Uncle Aerling at that same age . . . but in temperament, he is the spitting image of you." There was a twinkle in his eye when he said it. "Practically lives in the church, he does."

"At three years old? That's impossible, Holbodi."

"You did, my lord." Erlend's friend turned to the other Chieftain and winked. "Perhaps Lord Magnus cannot remember, but we old fossils do, don't we, Tor?"

"Indeed. I daresay young Rognavald Kolson has inherited much from his good uncle. We shall have to keep a close eye on him, shan't we, Holbodi? Obviously sanctity runs in the family."

"Oh knock it off, you two."

But what instantly amused Magnus was the memory of Aerling and Kol together that day in the cargo-hold. What would've they said if they had known they would someday become brothers, even if only by marriage? The thought made Magnus want to laugh.

But steering the subject back to serious ground, he asked, "Are you really sure Hakon will not war against me if I return to the

Orkneys?"

"Not with Norway on your side, my lord."

Magnus felt so torn. Dufniall had no right to oust Hakon. The royal bloodlines went through Erlend and Paal, not through Dungad. Magnus would be happy to help Hakon and bury their past, if only his cousin would let him. But at the same time, he was reluctant to leave this hidden and tranquil existence here in Scotland which he had grown so used to. Everything in him rebelled against going back into that world of power and greed and warfare. All he felt drawn to was prayer. Like his little nephew Rognavald.

"I'm afraid I need time to think about this."

"How much time, my lord?" Tor pressed. "War is on the horizon and the nobles are anxious for your return. Blood has already started to flow."

"Please, my lord. We are begging you. Sail with us."

Magnus knew, deep down, that he could not refuse. This was God's will and he must accept it. God had already asked of him very difficult things in these years since Berrfott's invasion. He had learned to welcome the Cross, although it was never easy.

"Alright," he finally agreed. "I will come"

The Chieftains looked immensely relieved. "We can sail as soon as you are ready," Tor said.

An old sadness resurfaced in Magnus's heart. "Just give me an hour," he requested. "That's all I need. I want to say good-bye to my wife."

It was their turn to be surprised. He couldn't blame them. After so many yearnings to enter a monastery, even he himself had been greatly surprised ten years ago when he had fallen so helplessly in love.

The Chieftains exchanged a delighted look. "Why didn't you

tell us you are married, my lord?" Tor exclaimed.

Holbodi asked, "Why say good-bye? Your good wife can come to the Orkneys with us. We will keep her safe from harm. You know we will."

"She can't come," Magnus told them, still feeling the sorrow which, even after years, refused to go away.

"Why not?" Tor asked, confused.

"Because," Magnus answered, "she's dead."

Mairee had died young, and she had died childless. Yet Magnus could not leave these shores of Scotland without one last visit to the grave of her who had never known anything but untouched purity, and who had thus won over so completely the young heart of the Orkney heir.

Chapter Twenty-Eight

"I wonder," Hakon mused out loud as he stared into the embers of the dying campfire, "if they have found him yet."

Sitting across from him, Ofeig looked up from his own wandering thoughts. "Which one?" he asked, not particularly interested. "Thorbjorn or Dufniall?"

Hakon took another swig of the mead in his horn and drained the contents. "Neither. Everyone knows where those two are. They've slunk off to the Shetlands to raise an army to bring me down. But they won't get away with it." He wiped his mouth across his sleeve and tossed the empty vessel angrily to the ground. "I'm talking," he answered the question, "about Magnus."

There was no one else around, just the two of them. All the other men had retired to their tents for the night. It was late and war had a way of grinding folks down.

"If he's going to get here," Hakon continued, "then I wish he would do it mighty quick. I need him and I need him right *now.*"

Ofeig quirked an eyebrow, wondering if his cousin had had too much to drink. "Uh, hold on a minute," he ventured. "Are you saying that you actually *want* Magnus to come?"

"You bet I do. And for more reason than just one. I can't wait till he gets here."

"Hakon, you're drunk. Go to bed."

"I'm not drunk, you idiot."

"Really? Then I think you need your head examined. You've

just spend the last thirteen years of your life madly wishing Magnus was dead, and now, out of yonder wild blue, you want him to return as the second Jarl. What on earth has gotten into you?"

"War, Ofeig! That's what's gotten into me. War."

"Alright, alright. I'm not saying you don't have any problems. But to want Magnus to come back? I don't get it."

"There is a huge difference," Hakon explained, "between wanting and needing. I am not going to lose the Orkneys a second time just because of two rotten scheming scoundrels like Dufniall and Thorbjorn."

Ofeig still didn't understand. "Even if Tor and Holbodi manage to find him," --- and everyone knew they were looking --- "what makes you so sure Magnus will side with you at all?"

Jarl Hakon did not even have to think. All he said was, "Don't be so stupid, Ofeig. Magnus loves these Isles. You better believe he'll defend them against a pair of insurgents. He knows full well that Dufniall has no claim to our grandfather's throne."

Valid point. Ofeig knew Magnus would fight, provided the cause was just. And this one was, no question. But they already had plenty of manpower. "So what difference," he asked Hakon, "will one more measly sword make? Magnus might fight, but why bother with him at all?"

"Because."

Ofeig waited, but Hakon left it at that.

"Because what?" he finally asked.

"Because . . . my obnoxious little cousin can do one thing I can't, and I need it to win this war."

Now Ofeig perked up, all ears. This was a breaking moment in history. Hakon Paalson was about to admit there was something he could not do. Unbelievable.

"Well, are you going to tell me, or are you just going to leave me hanging? What is this stupendous talent that Magnus possesses and you don't?"

For a long moment Hakon just glared at him, unwilling to admit it. Then he looked away and muttered, "He can inspire our warriors and lead them to victory. I can't do that."

The answer took Ofeig by surprise. "You're saying you need Magnus for *morale?*" He laughed outright. "Now I know you're drunk."

His cousin the Jarl gave him a look which, in a more sober moment, might be quite lethal. "Yes," he snapped, "I need him for precisely that. And if you understood anything in the least about war, you would want him here too."

Rebuked, Ofeig tried to look serious.

Hakon angrily continued. "Don't ask me why, but there has always been something about my cousin that makes people love him. By the way, I'm talking about *him*, not *you*. Personally I hate him, just as I hated his brother. But that shall be dealt with later. For the present, with Magnus at my side our warriors will follow us to the ends of the earth . . . or at least to the Shetlands, which is good enough for me."

Thinking about it, Ofeig had to agree. There was undeniably something about Magnus that drew others to him. Even Ofeig himself had at times, in years past, fallen under the spell. It was almost impossible not to like him, and even harder to understand why Hakon despised him so deeply. Aerling had been a different story, yes. But Magnus? How could anyone hold a grudge against *him*?

Hakon abruptly stood up and kicked some dirt on to the smoldering fire, the sign that their conversation was over.

Ofeig too rose from his place. Not out of respect for his Jarl, but simply because he was tired and wanted to get to his tent for some sleep. "This war could go on for years," he warned. "Are you really willing to rule with him that long?"

"I will rule with him for exactly as long as it takes. Not one day less, not one day more. But this war won't go on for years, Ofeig. Not once Dufniall and Thorbjorn find out what the *real* Orkney Jarls are made of!"

"What's the other thing?"

"Huh? What other thing?"

"You told me that you want Magnus to come back for more reason than one. To fire your warriors is the first. So what's the second?"

For the first time Hakon actually smiled.

"Why, to murder him afterwards. What else?"

Chapter Twenty-Nine

(The Shetland Islands, eight months later)

"Your weapons please, my Lord Jarl."

Magnus paused at the entrance of the hut and dutifully removed his sword. He handed it over, and the guard, a giant of a man, put it aside with the others.

"Anything else, my lord?"

"Yes. I have a hunting knife."

"I'm afraid I will need that too."

"Of course." Magnus unsheathed it from his belt and relinquished it as well.

"Is that all?" The man looked apologetic. And awfully cold. These Shetland nights brought with them the icy winds from the arctic.

"That's all," Magnus assured him. "But you must be frozen, Slund, standing out here half the night. I wish I could send you back to one of the tents to warm up a bit. I don't understand why the Chieftains won't let me."

The guard did his best to smile. "Duty is duty, my lord. My post is an honor."

Magnus knew the Assembly of Chieftains had made this rule explicitly for his own protection. No one was allowed to enter with arms whenever the two Jarls met together for anything. Including ---especially including---Hakon and Magnus themselves. The Chieftains would keep peace between the two, no matter what the cost or how drastic the precautions. And Slund was one of those precautions.

Our fathers didn't need all this, Magnus thought sadly every time. *Hakon and I shouldn't either.*

He glanced at the other weapons the goliath Slund had in his keeping and asked, "Who's in there with him?"

"Just his standard-bearer. No one else."

Magnus nodded. Ofeig. Never hurt to check beforehand.

Then Slund added, "The Socks should be returning soon. Within the hour, I would guess."

"Did you say . . . the *Socks*?" Somewhere within him, an alarm went off. A rather big alarm. "You mean, Sihvat and Gurd?"

"Of course, my lord. Who else?"

Magnus frowned. "I didn't know they were here."

"Well, they were earlier in the night."

"In the Shetlands, I mean."

The guard merely shrugged. "It's a big army, my Lord Jarl."

"You're right. We do have a lot of men."

But . . . Gurd and Sihvat were actually here? This was news. They had not been here a few days ago. Of that Magnus was sure.

'I bet you anything it was the Sock brothers,' Aerling had told him after the burning of Helge Stianson's farm. *'Grida thinks so too.'*

Slund was looking at him curiously. "Is something the matter, my lord?"

Magnus hesitated. "No. No, of course not, Slund. Just thinking." He forced a smile and removed his heavy outer cloak. "It's a bit small, I know," he apologized, draping it around the shivering giant, "but we don't want you to be an icicle before morning."

Not giving the other a chance to protest, Magnus pushed open the door and stepped into the tiny shepherd's hut they were using as temporary headquarters.

It was dark in here, and hardly warmer than outside, but at least it was protected from the bitter wind. Ofeig glanced up from where he and Hakon were huddled together over a table, studying by dim lamplight a parchment spread out before them. Hakon didn't even bother. The standard-bearer rose to his feet and stepped back, vacating his stool for the second Jarl.

All Hakon said was, "I found it. The perfect spot. I told you I would."

Magnus went over and sat down next to him. As usual, there was a wall of granite between them. He looked down at the map in the flickering flame of the lantern. "Where?"

Hakon pointed. "Here. Right where my finger is. Just on the coastline off Burra Firth."

"Burra Firth? Are you sure?"

The simple words made Hakon bristle.

Ofeig said, "He's always sure. Get used to it, my lord."

Hakon tossed his standard-bearer an ugly look then said to Magnus, "If you think you're such a genius, then find a better place." He shoved the map towards Magnus. "You won't."

"I didn't say I could find a better place, Hakon. I only asked if you were sure. An awful lot of lives are depending on us and we can't make a mistake."

"I know what I'm doing, Magnus."

Maybe, maybe not. Magnus was not just going to follow blind. He took the map and studied it himself while Hakon fumed in silence beside him. Too bad. War wasn't a power game between them.

As he considered the place his cousin was proposing, he could not help but wonder what his father would have done. Or his brother. Hakon's plan looked sound enough, but Magnus said a prayer nonetheless in his heart for guidance. Blood was going to flow. They had better do the right thing before God Almighty, because there would be no second chances for those men who would die.

"Do you really think, Hakon, that Dufniall is out there?"

"I don't think. I know. If we can get our fleet through that firth before him, we are going to smear our second-cousin's innards all over the coast. One good strike, right there, and this war will be over by next week."

Magnus desperately wanted to believe him. He couldn't fault the plan. "Alright," he agreed. "We'll wait a couple more days for Thorbjorn and if he doesn't show up by then, let's sail."

"No," Hakon said. "We sail tomorrow, at first light. I've already given the order."

Magnus felt a flicker of annoyance. Hakon had had no right to do that. "Retract the order," he said, keeping his own temper in check. "We are waiting for Thorbjorn."

Hakon just glared at him.

Stalemate. Yet again.

But Magnus wasn't going to back down. "We can't leave. You know as well as I do that Thorbjorn may be coming to surrender."

Hakon rolled his eyes. "You believe that?"

"I don't disbelieve it. He's had a falling-out with Dufniall, and he would have to be insane to keep fighting us now. I think there's a very good chance he wants to come over to our side."

"I said, we sail tomorrow."

"And I said, we're waiting. I'm sorry, Hakon. I really am, but our troops aren't budging an inch until we know what Thorbjorn intends to do. That's the whole reason our army has been sitting out here freezing to death in the first place."

It was always like this. They couldn't be together for more than five minutes without Hakon opposing him. It seemed he did it on purpose every time.

Magnus sighed, unwilling to start another fight. There were already so many festering wounds between them. "Just two days. Please, Hakon. That's all I ask. Can we at least find out where Thorbjorn is?"

"I already know," Hakon announced, "exactly where Thorbjorn is. I have known his location for hours."

"You didn't tell me that."

Feigning innocence, Hakon merely replied, "You didn't ask me."

It was taking a real effort now to remain patient. Why could not the other Jarl understand how imperative it was to this war that they work together? Human lives were at stake. And lives also meant souls. Forcing himself to stay calm, Magnus asked, "You mean you sent out scouts?"

Hakon had the nerve to laugh. "I did much better than that, I assure you. Thorbjorn will never give the Orkneys trouble again. He's finished. And by the end of the week, Dufniall will be too. We sail tomorrow."

Magnus was frustrated. He knew he was missing a vital piece of the puzzle and Hakon was keeping it from him on purpose.

At that moment, Ofeig announced, "They're coming back. I can see them through the window." There was something in his voice that did not sound happy.

Magnus turned in his seat and looked. Just visible through the window-hole there was indeed a glow of approaching torches in the darkness, their flames dancing wildly in the wind. As he watched, two horses slowly materialized and their riders dismounted outside the hut. He listened. They must be talking now to Slund. There were a few low voices . . . a short burst of laughter . . . the sound of swords being unbuckled and forfeited to the guard.

Magnus looked back at Hakon questioningly. "Who are they?" he asked. But he suspected he already knew the answer.

"Oh, just a couple old friends. That's all." Hakon flashed Magnus his most charming smile.

Then the door opened with a blast of howling wind and they almost seemed to blow inside. Sihvat and Gurd Sock, in person. Gurd had to struggle a bit to get the door shut behind them, but when he did, the contrasting silence after the burst of wind reminded Magnus of a tomb. Was it because of the freezing gust they had just let it, or did he feel those sudden chills up his spine for another reason?

'I seriously hope for your sake,' Aerling had said, *'that it wasn't them.'*

That little alarm was getting louder. Magnus instinctively rose from his seat. He had better be ready for anything.

Hakon also stood up. He asked, "Is it done?"

"Oh yes," answered Sihvat. "It's done."

Gurd said, "He has already woken up in Hell, nice and warm. No more cold nights for him."

"Excellent." Hakon all but glowed. "Was he alone?"

"Yes. No one else around for miles."

Magnus didn't like the sound of this. Not one bit. He looked from his cousin to the Socks and back again. "What," he ventured to ask, "is going on?"

Either they did not hear him, or, more likely, all three chose to ignore him. Hakon was already motioning for the newcomers to come to the map.

Ofeig answered quietly, "Thorbjorn. He was hiding in a cabin a couple miles north of here."

Magnus stepped back out of the way as the two joined the other Jarl at the table.

"Hakon," he demanded, "tell me what they did to Thorbjorn."

It was not Hakon who answered him, but Sihvat. Tossing Magnus a sickly sweet smile, he said, "We torched him. Right in his little bed. Sleep tight, Thorbjorn. Sweet dreeeeeeeams."

They'd *torched* him?

Magnus stared at his cousin. "You ordered these men to do that?" he asked, horrified. "Hakon, that's . . . that's murder!"

For the second time, Hakon rolled his eyes. "Look, Magnus, did we want him dead, or didn't we? I thought you would be overjoyed."

Magnus couldn't believe his ears. "Thorbjorn was coming to make peace with us," he said angrily. He could not remember ever having been this angry in his life. "You had no right to kill him."

Hakon didn't deign to reply, but Sihvat looked Magnus in the eye and asked, "Do you have a problem with that, little lord Jarl?" It was a straight-up challenge and Magnus knew it.

His brother Gurd pretended to suddenly remember something. Whacking himself on the side of the head, he exclaimed, "Oh my, Sihvat. We plain forgot. Magnus doesn't like fires."

So it *had* been them.

"Now, now, children," Hakon chided, "let's all behave ourselves, shall we?" He changed the subject. "I found the place to strike. Take a look." The Socks turned their attention to the map. "Right here ---"

Ofeig gently coughed.

"--- just inland of Burra Firth. See where I'm pointing?"

Another discreet cough.

"If we bring our ships to this little dot ---" The three were leaning intently over the table.

Now Ofeig loudly cleared his throat. Magnus glanced at him; what was wrong with the man?

"--- Dufniall will be trapped between ---"

Magnus realized with surprise that the standard-bearer was trying desperately to get his attention. Bewildered, he followed Ofeig's gaze until it rested where Sihvat Sock's right hand should have been, but wasn't. It was hidden in the folds of his heavy cloak as he studied the map with the others. What on earth . . . ?

Suddenly Magnus saw it. A glint of steel. Sihvat had smuggled a knife in here! And Ofeig had actually warned him!

As if somehow sensing eyes upon him, Sihvat looked up. Magnus and Ofeig both quickly averted their gazes away from his cloak and the other returned his concentration to the parchment and whatever it was that Hakon was saying. Something about Burra Firth being the final battle, then going home to the Orkneys.

He'd brought in a weapon!

They're exactly the type to stab you in the back and dump you over a cliff-face. Watch those two, Magnus. I mean it.'

Yes Aerling, he thought, *I'm watching them now. Believe me.*

"Hey, Magnus," Hakon said. "I forgot to show you something." He was casually motioning to the right side of Sihvat. "Come look. The light's best just there." He glanced up at Magnus and smiled.

Great. Now what?

In that split-second as he hesitated, Ofeig quickly stepped over to the table. To Magnus's astonishment, the standard-bearer placed himself right next to Sihvat, so that Magnus himself could not possibly stand there.

"Aren't you going to show me too?" he asked, pretending to be highly interested.

Hakon gave him a look that could kill. "I already showed you, Ofeig," he said, just barely managing to control himself. "An hour ago. Now move out of Magnus's way."

"But, I forgot. Where is this Burra Firth place again?"

Sihvat stiffened and his eyes flashed towards Hakon with rage, as if to say, *Get this oaf out of my way.* But it was too late. Ofeig was parked there, examining the map with pure fascination, as if Burra Firth were the most interesting thing he had ever seen. It was obvious to everyone he wasn't going to budge.

Good man, Magnus thought. *Thank you, Ofeig.* Forcing a polite smile himself, he moved over to the other side of the table, as far away from Sihvat as possible, and asked as naturally as he could, "So, what's this you want to show me, Hakon?"

Everyone was silent. The air was charged, like right before an electric storm. Magnus could see fuming glances being exchanged as people bent over that stupid bit of parchment, which no one was looking at at all, except for Ofeig. Sihvat's hand moved a few hesitant inches. He was obviously calculating . . . undecided.

All of a sudden, Ofeig brightly suggested, "Hey! I bet Slund would love to see this too." Before Hakon could stop him, he loudly called out, "Slund! Come have a look at Burra Firth!"

The door opened and the colossal guard, somewhat baffled by the summons, stepped into the room, his own huge sword clanging at his side.

"Fantastic little place!" Ofeig raved. "Burra Firth! Everyone's talking about it!"

Magnus let out his breath. High time, he decided, to get out of this hut.

"Well, men," he said out loud, "we've all seen it now. If we're sailing in the morning, maybe we better try to catch a few winks." He turned innocently at his cousin and asked, "Don't you think so,

Hakon?"

The look he received was nearly a dagger-thrust itself.

One thing Magnus knew for sure . . . There was no way in the *world* he would be closing his own eyes tonight.

Chapter Thirty

F rom the moment Magnus first sighted the coastline off Burra Firth, he knew his cousin had been right. He really had to hand it to him this time; it was indeed the perfect place to strike. One more battle and, please God, the war would be over.

"There's no sign of Dufniall, my lord," said Tor with some confusion, as the two of them stood on the deck of the warship.

"There's not supposed to be,Tor. At least not yet." Magnus glanced at the Chieftain and added, "We beat him here. Just like Hakon said we would." He looked around with satisfaction at the other Orkney ships following them through the firth. The next twenty-four hours would be a day to remember. "Dufniall is hiding out there with his army. But once he comes marching over that rise, he is going to meet the surprise of his life."

"Yes, I imagine he will. What orders then, Lord Magnus, shall I give to our men?"

Magnus didn't even have to think. "Tell them," he said, "to do whatever Jarl Hakon says."

For the first and only time in his life, he trusted his cousin completely.

* * * * * *

The only sound that could be heard anymore across the bleak and devastated shoreline of Burra Firth was that of the doleful wind's moaning. Even the lapping waves seemed hushed as they raced upon the blood-soaked sands to wash over the bodies which littered the beach. Seagulls circled but did not caw; nature itself seemed shocked by the appalling violence it had witnessed this day.

Magnus walked alone through the slaughter, trying to pray but hardly succeeding. It was just too big to take in. Months of fighting and planning and camping through the cold and desolate winter, and at last they had actually smashed Dufniall's army, he and Hakon together. Never would Magnus have dared dream of this day. After everything that had happened over the last thirteen years --- from Grida's attack and Hakon's exile, all the way to Berrfott's death and Dufniall's rebellion --- at long last the Orkneys were secure in the hands to which they rightly belonged, that of the line of Thorfinn the Mighty. Many lives had been sacrificed, far too many, and Magnus knew sadly that Hakon had been the initial cause of it all. His father's death, his uncle's, Aerling's in the Menai Strait, all had come about through his cousin's treachery. Not even to mention the hundreds of other lives which had been affected. But Magnus had long ago forgiven Hakon and, despite everything, today he had reason to thank God. It was over. Truly over. Their kingdom had this day been won back.

It would take awhile to sink in.

He clutched his cloak tightly around him against that freezing northern blast which never went away. He hated this place. He hated war.

All the men on the beach were dead, or would be soon. Limp and bloodied and mangled they lay, a look of unspeakable agony frozen upon each contorted face. Here and there a priest moved quietly among them, praying and checking and, where a heartbeat was found, absolving from sin. For the first time since Mairee's death, Magnus found himself grateful that his innocent young bride was no longer alive. She could not have faced this life of violence, the wife of a Jarl, and God in His mercy had known it. She had been spared.

The surviving warriors had all made their way --- alone or with the help of others --- back to the ships, where they were doing only heaven-knew-what. Binding wounds, getting drunk, greedily dividing plunder. Or, in some cases, numbly mourning the loss of a father, a brother, a friend. Even out here, Magnus could hear on the wind snatches of their boisterous laughter and revelry on the boats. But he had no desire to join them. Their other Jarl could do that, and no doubt was. As for Magnus, he wanted to be alone.

As he walked through the human wreckage he wondered sadly what made the hearts of men thirst for power and riches and revenge --- all the things that drew them to take up arms and kill. What were the measly treasures of booty over which even now his men were bickering or brawling? What was a throne, a kingdom, a crown? Why could not God's children live in harmony, forgiving one another and loving one another, as their Divine Master had tried so hard to teach them over a thousand years ago? *Why?* He would never understand.

"Magnus?"

The voice came from behind. A little startled, he turned around.

"I mean, uh, my lord," Ofeig corrected himself. He was standing there alone, spattered with blood and filth. By the looks of it he also had not been back to the ship to get cleaned up. He must have been out here the whole time, just like Magnus had. A huge sword, heavily stained, was in his hand, but he was holding it loosely at his side. He seemed distracted and somewhat unsure of his ground.

There was a short awkward silence as he groped for some

initial opening. Then he nodded towards Magnus's sword, which, unlike his own, was safely sheathed in its scabbard, and said by way of compliment, "You're not bad with that thing. Not bad at all." He gave a little grin and risked adding, "Admittedly, not as good as your brother Aerling was, but, well, the rest of us are only mere mortals, I suppose."

"You're quite handy with a sword yourself," Magnus replied, keeping his eyes cautiously on the deadly weapon in the other's hand. Oh yes, Ofeig was a skilled fighter too. Miles better than most. And the standard-bearer wasn't the only one unsure of his ground right now.

There was another strained silence. Ofeig obviously wanted to say something. He hadn't come all the way over here just to praise Magnus's swordsmanship; there had to be another reason. Magnus saw him nervously lick his lips and glance towards the warships anchored in the distance. Despite the cold wind, Ofeig was starting to sweat. He looked back at Magnus and lowered his voice. "I can't be seen with you. If our mutual cousin catches me here, my poor head's decorating a pike by morning. I would rather keep it right where God put it. Attached to my neck."

He was not joking.

They both looked around for somewhere to go, out of view of the ships, but there was nowhere.

Magnus said, "This beach is too exposed. It's not worth the risk. Go. I can find you later, somewhere private if you want."

"It'll be too late by then. You know he wants to kill you, don't you?"

Magnus smiled wryly. "I've known that since the day the four of you burned Helge Stianson's farm."

"I mean tonight. The war is over. He plans to murder you this very night." Ofeig threw another anxious look in the direction of the ships and Magnus could tell he really was scared to be out here. He was talking rapidly now, urgently wanting to vanish from sight. "Listen to me. You have to find another vessel to get away from this place. I don't know what. Maybe some Shetlander has a fishing boat or . . . something. But don't sail with the fleet. Hakon has a henchman on every warship. Not just Sihvat and Gurd. There's others."

Magnus couldn't believe this. "Are you serious, Ofeig?"

"Yes. I don't know who they are. They could be anybody. If I were you, I would trust no one. I mean *no one*."

Tor, Magnus instantly thought. Tor and Holbodi. Those two he trusted.

And, incredibly, Ofeig.

"You saved my life once already, back in the hut. Why? And why are you risking that head of yours to warn me now?"

The question seemed to throw Ofeig completely off balance. He clearly hadn't expected it. He was silent a moment, then admitted, "I . . . I don't know."

Magnus would take that. "Thank you, Ofeig," he said. "You're a loyal subject."

"I really must go. I bet he's wondering where I am."

"Then hurry. I'm not stopping you." Magnus swiftly wiped the blood off his hand and extended it towards the other. "Thank you," he said again.

It was only then that Ofeig seemed to realize he was still holding his sword, standing here all this time with that huge dripping blade in his right hand. With an apologetic smile and a roll of his eyes at his own blunder, he shoved the weapon into its scabbard and firmly reached out to accept Magnus's handshake.

Magnus said, "Let's both pray we're still wearing our respective heads when morning dawns."

Ofeig let out a laugh. "You can say that again. It's not often I get on my knees, but tonight, well, maybe I will."

"Good. So will I."

They exchanged one last empathetic look, then Ofeig turned and hurried away, leaving Magnus alone with the dead on the godforsaken shores of the place called Burra Firth.

Chapter Thirty-One

(The Orkneys, several months later)

"You do realize, don't you," provoked Sihvat Sock, "what he's planning to do? He's going to destroy you, rip you to shreds, and steal your half of the kingdom."

Jarl Hakon looked first at Sihvat, then at Gurd, who had cornered him yet again in his courtyard, as they always did when he stepped outside alone. These smelly Socks had been hanging around his fortress like a load of dirty laundry and he was starting to get awfully sick of them.

"Stop telling me," he warned, "what I should do. My kingdom and my cousin are none of your business."

"They *were* our business," Gurd shot back, "in the Shetlands."

Hakon simply walked away.

They followed and blocked his path.

"You told me to kill him," Sihvat snarled. "You wanted him dead!"

Hakon said icily, "And you botched it nicely, didn't you?"

"Ofeig did!"

"So what? You still failed. Don't come fawning to me for your reward after all this time."

"Let me try again."

"I said, I'll deal with Magnus my own way. I don't need you."

Hakon knew they wanted the other Jarl dead for their own reasons. No doubt they wanted *him* dead too. If Hakon wasn't careful, these brothers were going to get out of hand awfully fast, just like Thorbjorn and Dufniall had. Only worse. Much worse.

"You don't even know," Sihvat threw in his face, "where Magnus is, do you? Admit it. He slipped out of your clutches in the Shetlands and you're so useless you haven't even been able to find him."

Now Hakon was getting angry. He tried to control himself. "I have no need to find him," he replied coldly. "I already know where he is and I've known all along."

It was a lie. All he had was rumors, like everyone else. The latest one had reached him less than forty-eight hours ago and he had yet to follow it up. The infuriating thing was that Hakon was sure some of the Chieftains knew exactly where the other Jarl was. But they were playing ignorant.

"Fine then," Sihvat challenged. "You know where he is? Then why isn't he dead?"

Hakon was silent.

"Where is he?" Gurd asked point-blank.

Hakon didn't have to tell them anything. He was the Jarl, after all. But he wanted to save face with these two, so he answered. "Paplay. That's where." It was the latest report and his source was reliable. He hoped.

Sihvat frowned. It obviously was not the answer he had expected. "Why Paplay?" he asked.

"Because," Hakon told him, relieved to know at least something they didn't, "his mother owns a farm there with her new husband and that little brat of theirs, Karl or Krud or whatever his name is. Magnus wanted to spend some time there and get to know them."

Sihvat stared at him for a moment, then he had the nerve to laugh out loud. "You have *got* to be joking. You actually believe that?"

"Yes," Hakon said dangerously. "I do."

Sihvat looked at his brother and said, "Hear that, Gurd? How touching. Off to little mama's farm. He can feed the duckies and pet the baby sheep. Doesn't it make your heart just melt?" He turned back to Hakon and his face hardened. "He went back to Scotland, you fool. He's gathering an army, to bring you down. You are *really* stupid, Hakon."

Hakon froze.

Scotland? Nothing like that had reached his ears!

Sihvat continued. "He spent ten years there, Hakon. Ten *years,* and Canmore had six sons. That's six very powerful friends, who apparently all treated Magnus like a brother. Have you forgotten all this?"

Despite himself, Hakon felt the beginnings of fear. The sons of Malcolm Canmore! This wasn't funny. Not funny at all. "Who said he's there?" he demanded. "Tell me who."

Sihvat rolled his eyes. "It's so obvious. Of course he's in Scotland."

Gurd said, "Either that or Norway. You seem to forget he has connections there too. That brother-in-law of his, the one who married Gunnhild, he's not small stuff, Hakon. He has money and influence and men. All the things needed to grind you to dust. Kol Kalison could invade these isles at a snap of Magnus's fingers. Ever thought of any of this?"

Hakon hadn't. The idea of Magnus raising an army to overthrow him had never crossed his mind. Whether or not Gunnhild's husband was truly that powerful, Hakon didn't know, but what he did know was that the three sons of Berrfott had backed Magnus's claim to the Orkneys. And the Norsemen were the last warriors on earth he ever wanted to mess with again. He had thrown himself straight into their jaws the first time, back when he was young and foolish, but he had learned a hard lesson, with plenty of scars to prove it. Norway was even worse than Scotland . . . and Scotland was disturbing enough.

Sihvat said, "Just be honest, Hakon. You don't have a clue where your cousin is or what he's doing. Want some advice? Either find him and kill him, or go slit your own throat. Because one of you is going to die."

Sihvat was right. Magnus Erlendson was dangerous. Very dangerous.

Maybe it was not such a bad thing after all, Hakon realized, that these dirty Socks were still hanging around this place. Like it or not, he might need them yet.

Foul stench and all.

Chapter Thirty-Two

"Mama! Mama!"

Lady Thora, widow of Erlend, turned from the door of the chicken coop to see her four-year-old son Karl come bounding towards her across the farmyard, his face flushed with excitement.

"Men coming! Lotsa men!" he blurted breathlessly as he dived straight into her skirt, toppling the entire basket of eggs she had been collecting. His eyes were wide with fear, his voice trembling. "And they gots swords!"

Thora felt her heart stop. "Men with swords?"

"Big, big ones!" Karl told her. "Like *this*!" He stretched out his arms as wide as he could.

Thora suddenly felt as if she could hardly breathe. She tried to stay calm, so as not to frighten her little one more. "Where are they, Karl?" she asked. "Tell Mama where you saw them." She pulled him closer against her, instinctively wanting to shield him from harm. But it was not Karl they were coming for. It was her other son.

"Over da hill." Karl pointed wildly. "They coming dat way."

"Do you recognize them, sweetie? Any of them at all?"

He shook his blond head vigorously back and forth. "No, Mama. They scary!"

"Do not be afraid. Everything is going to be alright." She prayed he could not detect the fear in her own voice. "You say they're beyond that hill? The one over there?"

He nodded, his eyes huge.

Her mind was racing. She must not panic. Not yet, anyhow. She said, "Mama is going to go meet them. I want you to try to find Papa, and your big brother Magnus. Can you do that, Karl? Can you be brave and do that?"

The word *brave* did it. The child took a deep breath and nodded solemnly, proud to be entrusted with such an important mission.

Thora urgently tried to think where her husband and son might be. Then she remembered. "Look in the barn," she told him. "They were there a little while ago." They had been trying to fix a broken wagon axle and could easily still be working on it. Lady Thora marveled at how her son the Jarl could help his stepfather with such a humble task, as if it were the most natural thing in the world he should be asked to do. But he didn't mind at all. "If they're not there," she added, "then check the stable. If you still can't find them, go straight up to the hayloft and stay there, quiet as a little mouse. Do you understand, Karl? Don't make a peep, not one tiny sound, and don't climb down till Mama comes to get you. Promise me this!"

Again, his fair head bobbed up and down. "I pommise, Mama."

"Good boy. Now go. Quickly!"

She watched him dash off in the direction of the barn, then removed her apron and laid it on top of the overturned egg basket. For a moment she just stood there, trying to calm the violent pounding of her heart. Then she smoothed down her dress, her hands shaking. With dread she hurried to the crest of the hill, trying to be as brave as her little Karl.

She shaded her eyes against the glare of the bright sun. Her heart started hammering again. Yes, there they were in the distance, a dozen or so warriors. They were definitely coming this way, just as Karl had said. She strained to see their faces. At first she could recognize no one, then she suddenly spotted Vost . . . then Thrap. Erlend's widow could never mistake those fierce two. Never. That pair alone was enough to strike terror into the stoutest of hearts. But the one in the rear, with that limp, looked a little like dogged old Grusp who should have been in the grave years ago and ---

Relief came pouring over her like a torrent. Holbodi was with them, her late husband's closest friend. She let out her breath and whispered, "Thank you, dear God. Thank you." The relief was so great she felt almost dizzy.

Whatever had brought these fearsome warriors to her isolated farm in Paplay, it could not possibly be to shed her second son's blood . . .

* * * * * *

Magnus listened quietly as the Chieftains told their disturbing news. They were all sitting now at the kitchen's long table, as his mother and little half-brother scuttled around with mead and meat and cheese for the hungry travelers. Next to him, his stepfather Zieggert sat stiffly, his face furrowed in a frown. He did not trust these visitors in his house, nor liked what they spoke. He was a simple farmer, not a man of arms, and the sooner they left the happier he would be.

Magnus could see his mother pause in her serving every now and then and cast him uneasy glances, and the more his men revealed the more worried her looks became, until she was courageously blinking back the tears brimming in her eyes. She had already lost her first husband and her first son; Magnus knew she did not want him to leave the safety of Paplay and go with these Chieftains.

Surprisingly, it was his stepfather who finally interrupted them and bluntly asked, "So what you're actually getting at, in a plain man's terms, is that Jarl Hakon is starting to gather forces to go to war against our Magnus? Is that what all this means?"

Holbodi smiled at him indulgently. "Yes, good sir, I'm afraid that's what it means. In a plain man's terms."

"But I don't understand. Magnus has done nothing to provoke him! Why would he just start a war over absolutely ---"

"Because," the elderly Grusp interrupted, "there are rumors. Someone has been spreading malicious stories about Lord Magnus's long absence from the Mainland. If only these things had reached our ears earlier . . . but, alas, we also were ignorant until recently."

"People who spread gossip," Holbodi said tersely, "always know exactly whom not to tell, don't they?"

Finally Magnus spoke. He turned to his stepfather and said, "This is nothing new. There's been . . . things between Hakon and me for years." He looked back at the others and asked, "So, what are the rumors? What am I supposedly doing?"

Holbodi was the one who answered, and he didn't look happy. "It is whispered in many villages, my lord, that you are bringing in the Scots --- or even the barmy English, can you believe it? --- to overthrow your cousin and secure the throne for yourself alone. The peasants, especially, are living in great fear. After Norway's invasion all those years ago they want no foreign warships showing up on their shores. As a result they themselves are gathering crude arms and are no longer sure if they can trust you. I am so very sorry to tell you this, Lord Magnus. They are but simple folk, who know you and your cousin only as names, and

195

names that carry power and shed blood."

Little Karl was looking up wide-eyed at his older brother. He tugged at his sleeve and asked anxiously, "Is it true? Is King of Scolland really coming to our *house?*" The idea pleased and terrified him at the same time, as did all those huge broadswords hanging at the sides of these strange guests in his parents' kitchen. His big brother was only in a simple tunic and work trousers, just like Papa, smeared with grease from the wagon wheel in the barn, and Karl obviously couldn't understand why Magnus wasn't afraid of these scary men as well.

"No, Karl," Magnus assured him gently, "no one is coming from Scotland. I promise."

The little boy looked immensely relieved, and a bit disappointed too.

"Karl," their mother suggested, handing him a bucket, "why don't you go fetch me some fresh water from the well?" She didn't want him listening to all this frightening talk. Unlike her other four children, Karl had not grown up with gleaming weapons on the wall and the idea of bloodshed as commonplace as a meal on a table. He was a farmer's son.

Magnus waited till he was gone then turned to Holbodi. "You and Tor promised me this would not happen if I came back with you." It was a reproach. "I warned you that my return would eventually spark off civil war."

"Forgive us, my lord. We did not foresee these vicious rumors. People also say ---" he looked compassionately at Erlend's widow and addressed the next part to her, "they say that your son is bent on revenging Lord Aerling's death." He returned his gaze to Magnus. "That is the other lie circulating the isles. Your vengeance. After all, everyone knew how things stood between you and your brother."

Magnus said, "Aerling forgave Hakon before he died. How could I do less?"

He saw the astonished look on his mother's face and knew she was stunned by his statement. And from her point of view, he couldn't blame her. How many anguished memories she must have of Aerling's hatred for Hakon and vice-versa. Magnus knew it had been the cause of her deepest grief.

"Yes, Mother," he assured her. "Aerling did forgive. I know he did. We were on that ship together, remember?" He had never told her, and never would, how her other son had died.

"So," his stepfather cut in, "now everyone thinks Magnus is the evil one."

"Not necessarily so," Holbodi explained to him patiently. "To the contrary, there are many who desire him to avenge the blood of his brother, who was the true heir. The way they see it, Hakon was exiled and is not really their Jarl at all. Lord Aerling, were it not for his cousin's treachery, would be alive and the one on the throne. If anything, the people will goad your stepson on."

"And probably," muttered the sullen Vost, "think Jarl Magnus a coward if he doesn't."

"So what we have here," Zieggert ventured, "is a lose-lose situation. No one wants war, but at the same time, they want war. Am I correct?"

"Yes, good sir. The whole thing has become quite complex indeed."

Magnus said quietly, "I would rather abdicate peacefully, right here and now with all of you as my witnesses, and leave these Isles forever, than to take up arms against my cousin." His gaze slowly traveled the room and he looked sternly at each of his subjects. "I will not spill one drop of blood of a single one of my countrymen. . . and neither will any of you. Do I make myself clear?"

The warriors remained silent.

"Answer me. Are my words clear?"

Holbodi sighed. "My lord, it is not as simple as you want to make it. Things have already gone much too far and ---"

"Then you should have told our son sooner," thundered Zieggert. This was his house after all!

Holbodi politely raised a hand to request the farmer's silence and continued to Magnus, "If you surrender your half of the kingdom without even a fight, as you are suggesting, then there is sure to be an uprising against Hakon. Heaven only knows what the people will do to him themselves. They may assassinate him --- lynch him, burn him, do whatever they think of --- because they will resent him for ousting you. We are dealing, of course, with mob situations. The common folk out there truly have no idea what is going on. They believe blindly whatever they hear, and take sides wherever the wind blows."

"So whatever I do," Magnus said angrily, "our kingdom is already split in half. I did not want this to happen, Holbodi. I should have stayed away in Scotland and let Hakon deal with Dufniall and Thorbjorn himself. What difference did it even make that I was there?"

That certainly stirred up the men. Instantly the kitchen exploded with voices. Yes, he'd been needed at Burra Firth! --- No they could not have won without him! --- Jarl Hakon only had victory because Magnus was at his side! --- They were all declaring it at once.

Finally, it was Lady Thora's husband, the peaceful farmer, who rose from his seat and slammed his fist on the table. *His* table! "What," he demanded, "would you have poor Magnus do? Give us an answer!"

The room slowly quieted and it was venerable old Grusp who

spoke. "Please, please. Let's not get upset. We believe we have come up with a workable solution, and we hope to stomp down these troubles before they turn into actual war. Which, unfortunately, is not far away." He looked then at Magnus and explained, "We propose a peace-meeting between you and your cousin. Are you agreeable to that, my Lord Jarl?"

"Of course I am agreeable."

"But it must be soon. Very soon. We thought immediately after Lent, perhaps Easter Monday, April eighteenth, when the graces of the Resurrection are still strong upon us."

"That's only a week away," Lady Thora exclaimed with dismay. She didn't want another son dead so soon!

"It's alright, Mother. God is in charge of everything." Magnus looked at his Chieftains and asked, "Where? Under what conditions?"

Holbodi said, "Egilsay Island. Jarl Hakon has no solid support in the few hamlets there. At least not yet. He's working on it, but for the present it is as neutral a place as we can find."

"The conditions," Grusp took over, "are extremely simple. No weapons, no warriors, no ships. Only small boats and two companions each --- whoever you choose, same for Jarl Hakon."

"It sounds as if you have already planned this down to the last detail," Magnus said.

"Actually, my lord, we have." Holbodi looked apologetic. "None of us want the Orkneys divided. You know we love our rough lands. If there is any way to prevent civil war at this late stage, we will do all we can."

So would Magnus. He nodded and stood up. The Chieftains rose with him.

"I'm sorry, Mother," he told her softly. "I guess it's time for me to leave."

She held back the threatening tears. "Shall I go fetch Karl to say good-bye?"

"No," he said. He didn't want to upset his little brother. Then he added, "On Easter Tuesday, I will come back, and Hakon with me, straight here to Paplay. You will be able to see for yourself, Mother, that everything is fine." He looked at the Chieftains surrounding them. "Tell this to Jarl Hakon," he ordered. "I want it as part of the agreement. We return here, both of us. The day after."

"Yes, my lord. We shall tell him."

Lady Thora drew in a breath, trying to be brave. "Do you promise me that, my son? That you truly will come home?"

"Yes, Mother. We will come back together, and everything will have been forgiven. This I promise you."

As he made the bold avowal, Magnus was not sure himself how it could be fulfilled.

But God knew. And He was almighty. All things would work unto good. It had always been the way with Him.

Chapter Thirty-Three

"I don't like this plan, Hakon. It's dangerous and it stinks." His cousin didn't even bother to look up from polishing his axe in the ship's armory. "Who cares what you like or don't like, Ofeig? You're not the one who sits on the throne."

"Maybe not, but if I were you I would comply with the Chieftains and meet with Jarl Magnus in peace. You know exactly what that means, cousin: no warships, no weapons, and only two men. Obey the Assembly in this. You have no choice."

Now the other deigned to glance up. "But I am the Jarl." He carefully ran a fingertip close to the edge of the axe-blade, checking for flaws. "I *always* have a choice."

Ofeig said, "Then you're making an unbelievably foolish one."

Hakon lowered the weapon and glared at him. "My other cousin is bringing in the *Scots!* What do you expect me to do, imbecile?"

"Sure, sure, sure. Apparently he's also bringing Henry from England and the three kings of Norway. Next thing we'll hear the Papal Army is sailing up from Rome, with His Holiness himself steering the barque. Just how big do you think you are, Hakon, that poor little Magnus has to gallop the globe just to take you on?"

He saw Hakon's eyes flare and wondered for an instant if he had gone just a bit too far. That axe, after all, was mighty sharp.

But all Hakon said was, "Are you turning coward on me, Ofeig? Because if you are, I will gladly find another standard-bearer. I don't need *you* to carry my banner of war, to Egilsay Island or anywhere else."

"Cowardice has nothing to do with this. We have no actual proof --- none whatsoever --- that Magnus has gathered an army against you. What we are talking about here is murder. Premeditated, coldblooded murder, and against a defenseless man. I will carry your banner to *war* any day, but I want no part of assassination."

Hakon rolled his eyes. "Oh, I see," he said sarcastically, "holy Magnus the Saint has asserted his pious influence over you now too, has he? Next you'll be crawling off to a monastery to do penance for your sins."

Ofeig was getting angry, but he knew must remain calm. He was alone with his foul-tempered Jarl in a room crammed with deadly weapons. Not a cozy place for an argument. He wisely backed down. "Alright, Hakon, let's leave religion out of this." He would never admit that, yes, for some inexplicable reason Magnus Erlendson did make him think a little more of God than he ever had before. But that had nothing to do with this. "All I said," he continued, "was that you're making a mistake. Can't you understand that to show up at this so-called peace-meeting with eight fully equipped warships and the men that go with them will jeopardize your own crown? Magnus has won the love of the people and you will make an awful lot of enemies if you slay him."

"I can't believe you are actually saying this, Ofeig. You talk as if you expect me to share this kingdom with Magnus forever. I only welcomed him back because I needed his help in the Shetlands, but he has served his purpose and now he must go. Before he destroys me first."

"You know what, Hakon? You're just plain sick."

"And *you* are the most disloyal kinsman a man ever had. Get out of my sight!"

Ofeig tried one last time. "Listen to me, at least once in your life. Forget your vengeance. With Magnus at your side you could strengthen this kingdom beyond anyone's wildest dreams. Look at Burra Firth, how the two of you together inflamed your warriors! Forget the sons of Canmore, Hakon. They're not coming, any more than the Pope is, or Odin the war-god with a mythical Norse army. Someone just made the whole thing up and you fell for it. You *wanted* to fall for it, because it finally gives you your excuse, after all these years, to murder an innocent man. Prove me wrong, Hakon."

Hakon couldn't. He didn't even try.

Ofeig continued, "You and Magnus were once friends, even if it was way back in your childhood. You managed to get along with him then. Granted, you could never have reigned with Aerling, but Magnus is different. Why can't you make peace with him and rule together, just as your grandfather Thorfinn the Mighty wanted? It could work out if you let it, and everyone can see that. Even me."

"Well I certainly can't. And neither, may I remind you, did Hiedawaart-the-Wise."

"Huh?" Ofeig was suddenly lost. "Hiedawaart the *who*?"

"Can't you remember? Hiedawaart-the-*WISE!* The old witch in Sweden all those years ago."

It took a second to register, then the memory flooded back in all its hilarious detail. Before Ofeig could stop himself, he exploded with laughter. "Oh *no!*" he whooped, "Don't tell me you're going to dredge up old gorgeous again." He couldn't help it. He just couldn't. "You mean the one who made soup with your hair? Surely not her again!"

It was just so funny.

But . . . uh . . . Hakon wasn't laughing, Ofeig noticed a bit late. In fact, the Jarl with the axe standing five feet away from him did not looked amused in the least. His eyes flashed with rage and Ofeig wondered suddenly if this was the side of Hakon that Aerling and Magnus had always known.

"Go right ahead and laugh, Ofeig. All you want." His voice was more dangerous than the other had ever heard it. "But her prophecy was real. I *will* become the sole ruler of the Orkneys and my sons after me, and nothing can stand in my way. Not you, not Magnus, not even Almighty God!"

Ofeig sobered instantly. "Don't talk like that, Hakon. That's blasphemy."

By the look in his eyes, Hakon could not care less. For some reason --- which was strange because Ofeig didn't normally pay any attention to the Gospels read by the droning monks at Mass --- a line jumped into his head about Judas at the Last Supper. *'And after the morsel, Satan entered into him.'* Judas, who could have been good. Who even *had* been good sometimes. Ofeig wondered with sudden surprise why on earth he was thinking about *that*.

Hakon said, "I cannot alter my destiny. No man can. I'm only fulfilling what the witch foresaw."

Something about the way he said it, so brutal yet so calm at the same time, sickened Ofeig. He wasn't even scared anymore of that battle-axe the other held. "Fine then," he told Hakon. "You believe so much in her ridiculous prophecy, do you? Then remind yourself of the rest of it. Maybe *that* will make you change your mind about slaying an innocent man."

Confusion swept across Hakon's face. "What on earth are you talking about?"

"You can't remember, can you?" Ofeig challenged. "Well I do. Old Hiedawaart prophesied more than just power. She said something about a crime."

"Shut up, Ofeig."

"It's coming back now, isn't it, cous?"

"I said, *shut UP.*"

Ofeig didn't. "She told you you would one day commit a heinous sin. Something so inhuman that you would hardly be able to atone for it. Ever."

"Leave me," Hakon thundered. "Get out. *NOW!*"

The standard-bearer didn't budge. "But you still believe murder is your destiny?"

Now Hakon blew up. "*I am the Jarl,*" he shouted. "Do as I command. *LEAVE!*"

Ofeig turned away in disgust. "Whatever you say," he answered. The added sarcastically, "My noble lord."

He made sure the door slammed hard behind him, as he left the Judas alone with his gleaming axe.

Chapter Thirty-Four

In all his years spent on the high seas, Tor doubted if he had ever seen calmer waters than those of this Easter Sunday evening. The little boat glided along, the gentle breeze bringing it easily towards the shores of Egilsay Island. Neither he, nor Holbodi, nor their Lord Magnus could have hoped for a better day to sail.

Tor knew they were early. Jarl Hakon would not be expected to arrive until Monday morning with his own two companions, whoever they might be. But Lord Magnus had wanted to spend this coming night in prayer before the Blessed Sacrament in the chapel near the place they would meet, and be able to assist at Holy Mass in the morning. Thus they had left the Mainland earlier today. Just the three of them on this little boat, all unarmed, as agreed. Tor himself had been uneasy about the arrangements, but the Assembly had dictated these terms, and both Jarls had solemnly promised to abide by them. There should not be any trouble.

Hopefully.

He and Holbodi had noticed that their Lord Magnus had been exceptionally quiet during the journey over, spending most of his time alone in prayer in the boat's one small cabin. He was perfectly calm, trusting in God's loving care with unshaken confidence, and Tor wished he himself could feel the same. But, alas, he didn't. He feared the worst.

His uneasy thoughts, as he stood on the deck gazing out across the crystal blue waters at Egilsay Island in the distance, were suddenly interrupted by a gasp of horror from Holbodi beside him.

"Oh dearest God!" the other cried out in stark terror. "Tor, look! Look at that wave!"

Tor spun in the direction that his friend was pointing and immediately saw the most incredible sight of his life. His heart all but froze in his chest. It was like something out of a nightmare, something surreal, something that could never happen in real life. A giant tidal wave was rushing straight at them across the perfectly still waters of the sea. Tor tried, petrified, to gauge its height. Forty feet, fifty . . . he could not be sure; it was enormous. It had come out of nowhere. These waters were deep; what they were staring at was absolutely impossible. Yet --- yet there it was, coming right at them!

Tor realized there was nothing they could do. The wave was racing towards them with fearful speed . . . another minute, if even that, and it would hit this boat and bring with it certain death. There was no escape; no way they could ever survive.

At that moment, Lord Magnus appeared on the deck, as if he had somehow sensed the change in the waters and knew of the wave. He looked slightly dazed, as if he had been pulled out of some profound and mysterious prayer, and Tor was shocked to see how peaceful his expression was in the face of such imminent doom. He took one look at the deadly wave and said, "Do not panic, my friends. We must put ourselves in God's hands."

Easy for *him* to say, Tor thought wildly, his heart hammering with fear. It was coming! They could hear the roar as the towering wall of water charged directly at them. The sound was deafening, terrifying.

"If we are meant to die," Jarl Magnus told them serenely,

"then God's Will be done. If we are meant to live, He will protect us."
Was he even *seeing* this? Was he crazy?

Then Holbodi screamed and Tor tried to make the sign of the
Cross, and the massive force of thousands of tons of water crashed
straight into the boat. There was a tremendous rocking and
pitching, and the world vanished into blackness with an ear-
splitting sound louder than a hundred claps of thunder. Tor's
mouth and ears filled with water; he could not breathe, he could
not see; he was flailing helplessly, not even sure for a moment
whether he was dead or alive.

Then, as suddenly as the tidal wave had hit, it raced on its
course past them and Tor realized with utter amazement that the
boat was still floating and all three of them, although soaking wet
and shaken, were completely unharmed.

No one could find words in their astonishment. They watched
the huge wave continue across the waters until it finally
diminished in height and strength, then simply sank and
disappeared, as if it had never existed. The sea was once again
tranquil, not even a ripple on its clear surface.

A sense of the supernatural gripped Tor and he knew that
whatever had just happened was in a realm of which human minds
could not even begin to fathom. The wave itself had been against
all laws of nature, and their survival was certainly nothing less
than a miracle. Tor, together with Holbodi, looked searchingly at
their young master, both knowing he already lived at times in a
supernatural world.

Tor asked, "Why, my lord? Is this an omen, foretelling disaster
on Egilsay Island?"

Magnus gently shook his head. "I do not know, Tor, but I tend
to think not. I believe God sent this as a sign that all men and all
things rest safely in His loving care. We should be dead right now,

all three of us. But we're not. It was simply not our moment to go."
Tor saw him gaze out at the rough and rocky island towards which
they were sailing, and Magnus added firmly, "Nothing can harm
us, *nothing at all*, unless our Father in Heaven allows it. You must
believe this, my friends. God is the absolute Master of our lives.
We will each die exactly when and in the manner we are meant to."

"So," Holbodi asked softly, "you are not afraid of tomorrow,
my lord? Of meeting your cousin alone and unarmed?"

"No, Holbodi. I am not afraid."

Chapter Thirty-Five

"*H*e *would,*" Hakon fumed, pacing outside the church door. "Leave it to our little saint to go and hide in the chapel all day. Just how many prayers does the coward have to say? We've been waiting out here half the morning."

From where he was sitting on the church steps, Ofeig looked up at his cousin. "Can you blame him? If I were poor Magnus, I would take sanctuary in the church too. For heaven's sake, Hakon, do you think he hasn't spotted all your warships over there? They're just a tad difficult to miss."

"If he were as brave as everyone makes him out to be, he would come out anyhow and fight me like a man."

"Oh sure. You're camped out here with an axe and an army, and he he's unarmed with two old men. What do you expect him to do, fight you with his teeth? Come on, Hakon, this whole plan of yours is demonic. It's plain as day that Magnus hasn't brought warriors. No Scotsmen, no Norwegians, no one. He came here to Egilsay for one reason only --- to make peace with you."

"Just whose side are you on anyhow?"

Ofeig said, "Guess."

Hakon stopped his pacing and suddenly studied something off in the distance. "Hey, someone's coming," he announced. "Look over there. Those fellows with the black hoods." His tone seemed to say, *See, he did bring men.*

At first Ofeig saw no one, then through the trees he glimpsed a group quietly approaching the church. Sure enough, they were dressed in black, their faces all but hidden by heavy hoods.

Ofeig laughed out loud. "So, you reckon that's Magnus's bloodthirsty army, do you? Ever seen monks before? They're coming for Mass, lamebrain."

"Wonderful. Mass. That's all I need. Magnus will stay in there forever now." Frustrated, Hakon heaved the heavy battle-axe over his shoulder and said, "I'm fed up with this. Let's go back to the ship and get warm. I'll post a sentry to see when he comes out."

"And if he doesn't come out? You can't murder him in there, Hakon. You know you can't."

"You think he's going to live in there for the rest of his life or what? He has to come out eventually, to eat or . . . or something. And when he does finally step out those doors, I will be ready and waiting, believe me."

Chapter Thirty-Six

L ady Thora stood back and proudly admired the beautiful job she and Karl had done. They had been working since the moment midnight had struck, bringing with it the end of the holiest of Sabbaths, Easter Sunday. Now the house was decked in garlands of wildflowers, the table was scrubbed, the earthen floor carpeted with fresh rushes. Even the walls were draped with the exquisite embroidered rugs that Erlend had long ago brought to her as gifts from foreign lands, which Thora had not unpacked in years. This was not a palace, and could never match the luxury she had once lived in as wife of the Jarl, but the humble farmhouse kitchen looked as magnificent as she and her young son could possibly make it.

She was tired. So was he. What did it matter? There was cooking to do now, loaves to be made, fresh cream to be churned into butter. News had spread throughout Paplay; other women were bringing in baking and baskets of fruit, eager to help. They were excited for Lady Thora, yet more excited for themselves and the honor about to be paid to their lowly hamlet. The two Jarls would be coming tomorrow! Not just one, but both . . . and coming to celebrate what the whole kingdom yearned and prayed for. At long last, after over a decade of strife and uncertainty, the Orkneys would have peace and everyone could breathe again.

Yet for some reason, Thora could not shake off the feeling that something terrible was going to happen to her second son. She had already lost her first, and that sadness would never go away. She didn't even know how Aerling had died, for Magnus simply refused to tell her. Because of that, Thora knew it must have been awful. Would she go through it again and lose another child?

But although Magnus had not told her how his brother had died, there was something else he had confided to her. She thought of it now as she stood in her decorated kitchen, with its flowered wreaths and bright colorful hangings, and little Karl asleep on a pile of blankets in the corner. Magnus had assured her, incredibly, that Aerling had forgiven Hakon. If anyone else had said that, she would have found it impossible to believe. But coming from Magnus, it had to be true. He would never lie to her. And no one had been closer to Aerling than he had.

The remembrance of his words gave her sudden courage. If Aerling had accepted God's grace and forgiven, then maybe Hakon would too. Perhaps Thora was worrying needlessly. After all, Magnus had not been afraid to go and meet his cousin unarmed. He would not have gone if he thought it was a trap. Besides, if anything went wrong, Tor and Holbodi would be there. Surely they would protect him.

Yes, she told herself firmly, all would be well on Egilsay Island. Even now, this very moment, her beloved son and her nephew were being reconciled, and tomorrow would dawn the happiest day and the biggest feast Paplay had ever known.

Both Jarls would come together and all would be forgiven.

Magnus, after all, had promised her.

Chapter Thirty-Seven

Gurd Sock announced, "Here comes your sentry, Hakon."
"About time." Hakon growled. "If Magnus stays in that chapel any longer, we'll be nothing but a pile of old bones rotting on this beach."

He headed forward to meet the messenger, followed by a small group of his men. Most had remained in the warships, confused now and having misgivings. They had come to fight the vicious Scots, so . . . *where were they?* Where was this infamous kilted army waiting to do them battle? Word was spreading fast that Jarl Magnus had come alone, with no more than two unarmed companions. Hakon's warriors were baffled. What was going on?

But Hakon had no need now of their help. In fact, it suited him just fine if they stayed on board, out of his way. The less chance of interference, the better. After all, one never could tell when a man might suddenly change sides and decide to play the hero. A handful of trusted henchmen, loyal to Hakon's cause, would be plenty to achieve what he had come to do.

Sihvat and Gurd had been prowling the shore all morning like a pair of ravenous wolves. They had their own vengeance planned for Magnus, and had been yearning for this day since the burning of Helge Stianson's farm. Hakon knew they were taking it for granted that they would go with him as his two companions. But they were in for a big surprise. Hakon didn't want them. Tough.

214

He was going to do this his own way. Like it or not, the grubby Socks were staying behind.

He looked around the small group. "Where is Ofeig?" he asked.

Someone said, "On the ship with the others."

"Go get him."

"Yes, my lord."

A man went.

Sihvat looked startled. Hakon saw the glance exchanged between him and Gurd, and he could read their minds. Yes, yes, he knew perfectly well that Ofeig had been the one who prevented Sihvat from killing Magnus months ago. That's precisely the reason Hakon wanted him now. Let the Socks wonder and fume. He didn't care.

The party reached the approaching sentry. "What news, my man?" Hakon asked.

"Jarl Magnus has just left the church. He is heading to the place designated by the Assembly."

"Excellent. And Tor and Holbodi? Are they with him?"

"Yes, my lord."

"Armed?"

"No. At least not that I could see. They may be hiding weapons."

"I will take precautions." Hakon wasn't worried. Even if they tried to cause trouble, which was unlikely, they were vastly outnumbered.

Sihvat spat out, "Here comes Ofeig. Don't tell me you're taking him."

Ofeig was obviously just as unhappy as Sihvat and Gurd. Well, tough for him too.

"Hakon," he said, arriving, "don't do this. It's outright murder. There is still time to change your mind. The witch's prophecy doesn't have to come true."

"Shut up, Ofeig. You're coming with me. I want you as one of my two companions."

Ofeig was stunned. He hadn't expected this. Like everyone else, he had automatically assumed it would be Sihvat and Gurd. "No," he said flatly. "I will have no part of this. I've already told you that. Leave me out of it."

Hakon had no actual proof of course that his standard-bearer had purposely saved Magnus that night in the hut, but he had very strong suspicions that Ofeig had seen that hidden knife on Sihvat and had acted accordingly. Hakon would have his revenge today on not only one of his cousins, but *both* of them. "I said, you're coming with me. You and Lifolf."

Ofeig instantly looked bewildered. He frowned. "Lifolf? Who on earth is Lifolf? Never heard of the man in my life."

"He's my cook, moron. The man who fills your ugly gut."

Everyone, in fact, looked dumbfounded. Perhaps nobody knew who the poor fellow was.

It took a moment or two for Ofeig to even picture the man, but as soon as he did, he could not help himself. He let out a whoop of laughter. "You've got to be joking. You can't possibly mean that baby-faced individual who looks like a squished cherub? What do you want *him* for? To fry Magnus a couple of eggs?"

"I'll have him fry you, Ofeig, if you're not careful. Don't you know anything about anything? Lifolf is innocence itself. Magnus will take one look at him and know I have come in perfect friendship."

Ofeig instantly sobered. Maybe it wasn't so hilarious after all.

"Sentry," Hakon said with a smile, "be so kind as to fetch me Lifolf-the-Lily. I have great need of my gentle cook. Now."

Chapter Thirty-Eight

"He brought an army with him. The devil! What are you going to do, my lord?"

Magnus said, "I'm not sure, Tor. There's not much I can do. Looks like we're trapped." The three of them could not even make it back to their own boat if they tried.

They had reluctantly left the chapel after Mass, and were now waiting at the spot in the woods designated by the Assembly where the two Jarls were to meet. Magnus could not help wonder if his Holy Communion and the confession he had just made would be his last. "Maybe," he ventured, "once Hakon realizes we are truly unarmed and alone, he will change his mind and agree to make peace. That's the whole reason this was arranged in the first place."

"Well," Holbodi said, "we're about to find out. Here he comes now."

Magnus watched the little party approaching through the trees and was stunned to see that, yes, Hakon had only two companions. He was even more surprised to see who they were. It was not Sihvat and Gurd, as he expected. No, it was some chubby stranger with a face like an angel . . . and simply Ofeig. The first looked unable to hurt a flea, and the latter had long ago won Magnus's trust in the Shetlands. In fact, Hakon's choice could not have been less threatening. All three were obviously unarmed. Apart from the strange fact that his cousin was wearing such an unseasonably heavy winter cloak, the trio looked perfectly harmless.

Tor said quietly, "Everything is as it should be. Thanks be to God. Maybe he will abide by the rules after all."

"So," Hakon said when they arrived. "We meet at last."

Ofeig and the cherub moved to the side, as did Tor and Holbodi. The four were not allowed to interfere and they knew it. They were only here as witnesses.

"You have been gone, Magnus, a very long time from the Mainland. I have not been happy about that."

"I have been in Paplay," Magnus said, "not raising an army against you. I never went to Scotland, or Norway. They were lies, Hakon. All I have ever wanted was to put the past behind us and make peace. You know I speak the truth."

"I am sure you do," Hakon replied. "But, see, Magnus, we have a little problem. We always have. Poor grandfather may have been Mighty, but he was stupid and could not count. Two Jarls in the Orkneys is one entire Jarl too many, and I am afraid one of us will just have to go." His eyes traveled for a split-second to something in the dense trees beyond, and he made an almost infinitesimal motion with his head.

Someone, Magnus suddenly realized, *is out there. God, at least protect Tor and Holbodi!*

"I am happy," he said, "to leave forever. The kingdom can be yours, Hakon. Let me return to Scotland, and I solemnly promise I shall never set foot in the Orkneys again."

"Scotland! Hah! Never there, cousin. No way."

"Then I will go to the Holy Land instead, and spend the rest of my life doing penance for both of us. Will that solve our problem?"

"Forget that. I don't need your pious sackcloth and ashes."

Magnus tried again. He had to protect his two Chieftains!

"Then throw me in prison if you must. I just beg you, Hakon, let us come to some agreement, without bloodshed."

To the side he could see that Tor and Holbodi were tense. They did not at all like the way this conversation was going. Neither, by the looks of it, did Ofeig. The fourth man simply appeared bewildered, as if he did not understand why he was here or what was going on.

"We're cousins," Magnus persisted. "We're blood! Why can't we just bury the past, all of it, and finally make peace? We were once friends, Hakon, you and I, back in our childhood. I know you remember. For heaven's sake, our fathers were brothers. Let us be so too, as much as we can."

"Peace. Is that what you truly want, Magnus? I mean, *truly*?"

"Yes. Of course it is."

"I can think of one way to end in peace. But only one."

"Then tell me. I promise I will do my best to comply."

Hakon smiled. "I want you dead." Then his face darkened and he ordered, "On your knees, Magnus. Get down! *Now*."

That was it. Tor and Holbodi moved fast, but not as fast as the six hidden warriors who sprang out of nowhere and grabbed them from behind. Before anyone knew what had happened, the two Chieftains were held at sword point and the Jarl produced an axe from beneath his heavy cloak.

Everyone froze.

The angel nearly fled in panic. Ofeig looked furious, as did Holbodi and Tor. But none of them could do a thing. They were unarmed and outnumbered.

"Kneel down!" Hakon ordered a second time. "After all, that's your favorite position isn't it?"

Magnus hesitated. "Tell me first what you will do to my friends. Will you murder them too?"

"They will live or die depending on your cooperation."

Magnus instantly went down on his knees. "Hakon," he said, kneeling before him, "do not commit this sin. I have already offered my life to God as a sacrifice, should He accept it. But if my death comes by your hand, you will be plunging your own soul into Hell. I beg you, not for my sake but for your own, do not slay me in cold blood."

Amused, Hakon glanced around at the others. "Hear that, boys? Saint Magnus is preaching us a little sermon."

Ofeig said, "Let him go!"

"Oh just shut up, Ofeig." Hakon looked down on Magnus and smiled sweetly. "You have greatly misunderstood me, my poor cousin. I have no intention whatsoever of slaying you in cold blood. In fact, that is exactly why Ofeig has come. He shall do it for me."

He held out the axe to his standard-bearer and said, "Payback time, Ofeig. His blood can be on your hands."

"*WHAT?* You're out of your mind!"

"So you refuse to obey, do you?"

"You bet I do!"

"You're going to regret your decision," Hakon warned him. "But not as much as Magnus will, I assure you. He will wish more than anything that you had taken this axe."

Ofeig had no idea what he meant. "Never," he said.

"Are you *positive*? Last chance."

Ofeig's face gave him all the answer he needed.

"Well then, Lifolf," Hakon announced, "I'm afraid it's up to you. You're the cook. Surely you're used to butchering meat." He again held out the axe.

The man looked ready to faint. "You --- you want me to k-kill Jarl Magnus?" he stammered. "N-never, my lord. I can't! I --- I won't!" He helplessly sought an escape, but there was no place to run, not with these six fierce warriors surrounding them.

"Does no one obey me?" the Jarl shouted. "Do it, Lifolf, or you'll be some wolf's supper tonight! I mean it."

Magnus said from his humbling place on the ground, "Lifolf, obey him and take the axe. The sin is not yours. God knows you act against your will."

The terrified cook stumbled over and accepted the huge blade in his trembling hands. He really looked ready to die.

Hakon was satisfied. "Good," he said. "We can finally begin."

Begin?

Magnus suddenly realized his cousin had something all planned out. For the first time, actual fear began to creep over him.

"There are several ways," Hakon informed the group, like a showman addressing an audience, "to execute a man with an axe. Magnus here, I have no doubt, knows all of them."

Oh yes. The other Jarl certainly did.

Tor urgently tried to free himself. It was no use.

"Yet our good friend Lifolf," Hakon continued, "is only a simple cook. He has never had to slaughter a man in his kitchen --- only an ox or a sheep." He looked down at his victim. "So why don't you explain to him, Magnus, exactly how it's done? We don't want him, after all, to make any painful little mistakes, do we?"

Magnus remained silent. His heart was starting to race. He had already encountered an axe-blade once in his life and the experience had been anything but pleasant. But that time it had been in the midst of battle when he was full of adrenalin, which had a marvelous way of taking away fear and had even kept the pain at bay for a short while. He remembered how he had not even realized the extent he'd been wounded until his brother had pointed it out. But this was different. Completely different, and Magnus realized he was afraid. He was not afraid to go to his God, yet he was afraid, as is all humanity, of that terrible last moment before going.

"Tell him, Magnus," Hakon again said, indicating towards Lifolf with that giant weapon shaking uncontrollably in his hands. "How do you officially kill a man with an axe?"

Still no answer. *Help me, Jesus,* Magnus prayed. Even He had been terrified in the Garden.

Finally Hakon shook his head, as if he were a disappointed teacher dealing with a naughty little boy. "Alright," he said patiently, "I will help you get started. Explain to Lifolf only the way we are presently concerned with. The way one would, for example, execute a criminal, a common man, or . . ." he paused, pretending to think, "or an insurgent. One who tried unjustly to take another's throne. Tell him that one, Magnus. Go ahead. I know you know exactly what it is."

Magnus realized there was no way out of this. The lives of Holbodi and Tor depended on his cooperation; Hakon had made that clear. So he answered, "You would behead him."

The pleased schoolmaster beamed. "Excellent! You would behead him! Yet that can be accomplished in more than one way. Either by putting the fellow's head upon a block and chopping down, like cutting meat. Or, if one is extremely skilled with his axe, he could dispense with the block altogether and simply. . .do what?"

Keep answering, Magnus told himself. *Just get through this.*

. "The executioner," he replied as bravely as he could, "would just swing his axe and slice the head off the body."

"Excellent again! The type of thing I'm sure you yourself could do with your eyes closed."

His cousin was actually enjoying this. *God have mercy on him,* Magnus prayed. *Forgive him, dear Lord.*

"And the criminal would be . . . in what position?"

Holbodi angrily cried out, "That is enough. If you are going to kill him, you devil, than just do it quickly." He struggled to free himself, but the man holding him immediately pressed his sword blade directly against the Chieftain's throat.

"I asked you a question, Magnus. In what position would the offender be, in order to be beheaded by the swing of an axe?"

"He would be," Magnus said steadily, "on his knees."

Offer this up . . . Offer it up for Hakon's poor soul . . .

"Ah! Like you?"

"Yes, Hakon. Like me."

His cousin faked a frown. "But I seriously doubt that our gentle Lifolf is as expert an axeman as all that! He might make a rather messy job of it, requiring many swings to eventually severe your head from your body. During which time, I greatly fear, you may well remain conscious. What do *you* tend to think, Jarl Magnus? Could Lifolf do it?"

"I tend to think, Jarl Hakon, that he could not."

"Ofeig could have done it with one clean swipe, and you would not have felt a thing." Hakon tossed Ofeig a huge smile. "But too late now. For both of you, my poor cousins."

Ofeig looked like he would love to do it to Hakon.

Magnus's heart was racing wildly. The *pain!* What was he in for? No ruler chose an executioner who could not do his job!

"But guess what!" Hakon cheerfully announced. "Monday must be your lucky day. For, as earlier mentioned, only a commoner, a thief, or one who tried to take a throne which was never his by right, would be beheaded in the first place." He laughed. After all this! "And unfortunately for you, son of Erlend, you are none of those."

Everyone out there was blazing. Except Hakon. And maybe his six thugs.

"So let's move on and explain to Lifolf an entirely different way, the most *terrible* way, to execute a man with an axe. The one reserved for those nobly born --- kings, princes, and . . . why yes, I suppose Jarls. Describe to him *that*, Magnus." His eyes hardened with almost demonic hatred. "The way you and I used to play it when we were little boys."

"Hakon," Ofeig said, "stop it. Are you possessed, or what?"

Jesus . . . Jesus . . . I am so frightened.

"Go ahead, little cousin. Don't tell me you've forgotten all the fun we used to have together? Until, of course, you would always go whimpering off to big brother and make him spoil everything for us."

Magnus wondered, *Will this poor man save his soul?*

"Tell him, Magnus, or your friends die."

Magnus looked up at Lifolf, who seemed more terrified, if possible, than himself. The cook had even started to cry, huge tears rolling down his baby cheeks. "Do not weep, Lifolf," Magnus said kindly. "It is not manly. It is he who gives the order who commits the sin."

"You're right," Hakon finally agreed. "Your death is *my* honor alone. I have been waiting for this day for years, and I gladly take your blood upon my soul."

Magnus could not bear to look at him anymore. He offered his life for Hakon's conversion. As steadily as he could, he explained to Lifolf, "It is unfitting for a nobleman to be beheaded like a common thief. You must stand right in front of me and . . . and strike straight down . . ." he had to pause, hardly able to breathe, ". . . so that . . . so that my skull be split in half."

Everyone was deathly silent.

Ofeig, Magnus thought with anguish, *why didn't you take the axe?* Ofeig would have been merciful; he would have done it quick and clean. Hakon was right. They both regretted it now.

The harsh sound of Hakon's slow mocking applause cut through the silence. "Well done, Lord Jarl," he praised. "I could not have explained it better myself." He stopped clapping and said, "I can only imagine the nobleman at this point would pray his heart out that the fellow's aim was absolutely perfect, because if not, it wouldn't feel very nice, would it, Magnus?"

Suddenly, out of nowhere, Satan was there. *Hate him, hate him, hate him,* the serpent whispered in his ear.

It was hard to even breathe anymore from the fear, but Magnus managed to answer, "No, Hakon, it wouldn't feel nice at all."

"See, we do agree on a lot of things. Who says we don't?"

Animal. Animal! The temptation was suddenly very strong. *Despise him. Hate him for this!* The serpent's hissings were louder now, more vicious.

Meanwhile, the show over, Hakon was helping the blubbering cook position the shaking axe high above his head for the downward thrust which would shatter his skull. "Hold it steady, my man," Hakon was instructing, "until I tell you. And you heard him yourself --- don't miss."

'My man' . . . how dare he?! The poor fellow was in tears, actually crying in front of all these warriors! *What a fiend,* Satan said, *to do this to poor innocent Lifolf! And Ofeig too!*

Hakon stepped back out of the way. "Magnus," he ordered quietly. "Look up at me. I want to see the fear in your eyes as you die."

How dare he humiliate you, making you stay on your knees all this time like a . . . like a . . . coward! You don't have to take this from him! He's not even the true Jarl!

Magnus tried in confusion to push the thoughts away. *Go*

away, Satan! This was hard enough without him!

Lucifer instantly switched tactics. *He's not the Jarl, nor should you have to be either. You never wanted this job. It should have been Aerling. But Hakon murdered him. MURDERED HIM! Murdered your brother!*

It was true; Aerling's death had been caused by Hakon!

Hate him for it! Hate him!

No temptation in his life had ever been so violent! Magnus instantly felt his soul gripped in what felt like a stronghold of demonic hatred. He looked up; Hakon's face was like steel. The two Orkney Jarls locked eyes.

Grab the axe from Lifolf. Magnus froze at the idea. *Grab the axe and kill Hakon instead!*

It would be so easy! Ofeig was good with a blade; Magnus was better. He could have Hakon's head sailing halfway across this field in one clean swipe before anyone realized what had happened. And he wouldn't even have to get Hakon on his knees. *Jesus, Mary . . . he could do it! He could actually do it!*

But what about Tor and Holbodi? Their throats will be slashed!

They're old. They'll die soon anyhow. Besides, they would be so proud of you. You'll be a hero! The whole kingdom wants you to avenge your brother's death; they told you so themselves, didn't they?

No! No! It's a mortal sin!

God will understand. Is He merciful, or isn't He?

Oh God! He'd never been so tempted in his life! Magnus realized he was shaking, not from fear anymore, but from the intensity of the battle raging in his soul. It would be murder! True, coldblooded murder!

The horrific memory suddenly rose up in his mind of his brother's dead body, with that Norwegian sword impaled straight through his spine. It had been *Hakon's* fault! Hakon's treachery had killed him, more truly than any Norseman's blade. *Aerling would never hesitate to defend your honor, would he? He gave everything for you in that cargo-hold. Everything! Is this how you repay him, letting his killer get away with it? Is this how little you loved your brother?*

Go away, Lucifer! GO AWAY! This angel was too strong! He was going to win! *Grab the axe and slay him for your brother!*

"Any last words," Hakon asked him, "before Lifolf empties your brains all over the ground?"

Hatred was flooding through him in torrents, engulfing him, completely sweeping his soul in its tide. *Mother of God! I'm about to crucify your Son!* The axe *right there,* so easy to leap up and grab it from Lifolf . . .

Blessed Virgin, don't let me sin! Don't let me sin! Help me! Help me!

"So, no last words?"

"Yes!" Magnus cried out. These were the hardest words of his life, but he *wanted* to mean them! He *did* mean them, despite the screams spewing from Hell! "I forgive you, Hakon, with all my heart!"

In that instant Lucifer vanished in terror, and a deep and joyous peace swept over Magnus's soul. God's holy Mother, as always, had crushed the serpent.

Enraged by his parting shot, Hakon screamed at Lifolf, "Do it! *NOW!*"

Magnus quickly bowed his head. "Into Thy hands oh God I commend my ---"

The axe came down.

Chapter Thirty-Nine

"Hakon! Hakon, wait!"

The Jarl stopped in his tracks and turned to see someone in the distance running towards him. The beach was otherwise deserted; he had believed he was out here alone. Yet, who was this coming? The man was stumbling across the sands like one greatly agitated, racing and waving wildly. Whoever it was, he had obviously left the ship and gone back ashore this morning, although Hakon couldn't imagine why. The only reason he himself was out here was to check that Tor and Holbodi had departed without making trouble in the village. Thankfully, they had. And by tonight, all going well, Hakon too would be back home, far from this island of blood.

"Hakon! You'll never believe this! You've got to see!"

The rising sun was bright and it was hard to tell whom it was. The man was waving with one hand and clutching something in the other.

Hakon shielded his eyes against the glare, then recognized the figure. *Great. Bloody Ofeig.* It *would* have to be him. Hakon was tired and fed up, and felt more miserable than he ever had in his life. Ofeig was the absolute last person he wanted to face right now.

His cousin reached him, breathless and excited. "Look at this," he gasped, his eyes huge with some discovery. He didn't even seem to notice how annoyed the Jarl was. He was trying to catch his breath. "You . . . you have to see this."

"See what?" This had better be impressive. Hakon was in no mood for games. He watched like a martyr while his crazy cousin started to unwrap the cloth he was holding. He did it with unbelievable care, almost reverence even, as if its contents were the most costly thing in the universe. What an idiot. Hakon heaved an impatient sigh.

"Look!"

Ofeig was holding it out now, a handful of . . .

Huh? He must be joking . . . *Flower petals?* What on earth was he doing with a bunch of stupid ---

And then the fragrance hit him. He staggered back, almost knocked over by the scent that came from within that little cloth. It was unlike anything he had ever smelled before --- so impossibly lovely, so heavenly, that it could not belong to this earth. The celestial aroma instantly surrounded them, enveloping them in its sweetest perfume, so delectable that Hakon could only stand there stupidly like Ofeig and stare at the petals with astonishment.

Then he noticed how incredibly beautiful the flowers themselves were. White as the virgin snow, each petal was perfect and flawless; they were simply the most beautiful and exquisite thing he had ever seen. Before this moment no measly flower in the world could elicit from him even a passing glance, but *these!* They were spellbinding. It took a tremendous effort to tear his eyes away.

"Where?" he asked numbly. "Where did these come from, Ofeig?" There were no flowers growing on the barren, stony ground of Egilsay Island. Certainly none that he had seen.

Then Ofeig reached beneath his tunic and pulled out the

solitary blossom he had been hiding.

Its petals were crimson with blood.

Terror seized Hakon and his heart started to race. "No!" he cried. "Don't tell me, Ofeig!"

But Ofeig told him anyhow.

"They grew overnight, hundreds of them, right over the spot where Magnus's skull was shattered. Honestly, Hakon, they're everywhere! The ground is covered with them. You wouldn't believe!" His voice was unsteady with emotion. "After you took the body away last night, I saw a mysterious light from my window on the ship. It seemed the entire sky was filled with some strange beautiful glow, unlike anything I've ever seen, coming from the place you killed him. So I went out this morning to look and ---" Abruptly he stopped, seeing the horror in his cousin's eyes.

Hakon was paralyzed with fear; a sense of the supernatural gripped him. The heavenly fragrance wafted stronger and stronger around them.

But Ofeig simply could not stop. He had to go on with his wondrous story.

"There was a group of people there gathered from the village. Some old lady was born blind and everyone was all excited, saying she too had seen the heavenly light and instantly could see. Then a little boy with a crippled arm --- I witnessed this! He touched the spot where ---" His voice faded. Poor Hakon did not need to hear more of this. He looked like he was about to die.

For the first time ever, Ofeig knew when it was time to shut his mouth. He carefully folded the precious blossoms back within the cloth, and extended the bundle towards his cousin.

"Take them."

Hakon backed away, staring at the cloth with dread, unwilling to touch those flowers. His eyes held something close to panic.

"Take them, my Lord Jarl," Ofeig demanded. "His blood is on *your* soul. You said it yourself." He forcibly placed the sacred parcel into the murderer's ice-cold hands. "These did not grow here on Egilsay for the sake of an old woman and a lame child, Hakon, and you know it."

Yes, against his will, he knew it. These flowers had been sent from Heaven by Magnus, expressly for the one who had hastened his pure soul to such high glory.

Hakon was in trouble. Big, big trouble. And with God, of all beings!

Frankly, he was petrified.

* * * * * *

Lady Thora sat on the darkening porch, wringing her hands with anxiety. Her eyes were locked, as they had been all day, on the little hill over which any visitor to her husband's farm must pass. It was growing late now, dusk was falling. Where were they? Why had they not come?

The friends who had stayed on until the last hour had finally headed back to their own abodes, unwilling to travel the lonely paths after dark. The flowers bedecking her kitchen were limp now and wilting, the food had grown cold. All the barrels of mead had hours ago been drained by impatient and thirsty men as Paplay waited for the celebration that had never come.

Even little Karl had been too tired to stay up any longer and was tucked in bed soundly asleep, his disappointment soothed by Papa's promise that big brother would surely show up on the morrow. He had assured his wife the same. "Do not fret, my dear," he had told her, "they will come; you'll see. It is only a delay, nothing more. These things happen." Then he had kissed her, and yawned, and taken his weary bones to bed, convinced that nothing was wrong. He, after all, had not seen the things in life which she had.

Alone now on the porch, Thora sat on the rickety chair and tried not to panic. First Aerling, then Erlend . . . was her Magnus slain too? Had her nephew killed him, as he had long ago sworn?

Over and over she repeated in her mind the words her son had spoken. Was it only last week?

'Aerling forgave Hakon before he died. How can I do less? Yes, Mother, he did forgive . . . you have to believe me . . .'

Yes Magnus, she thought, I believe you, my son. She would cling to his words and hold them in her heart, no matter what the next hours or days would bring. She must not be bitter; she must not hate. Whatever had happened yesterday on Egilsay Island, she must treasure the example given by her own dear boys . . . and she herself forgive.

But please, God, let him be alive!

Suddenly she leapt to her feet. A solitary horseman was appearing over the crest of the hill. She strained her eyes in the fading light to see.

No one rode with him. He was alone, whoever he may be.

She realized her hands were starting to tremble. In fact, all of her was shivering. She wrapped her shawl tighter around her shoulders, even though it was not the air which caused the sudden chill.

It was . . . *that*. The strange load carried on the horse with the rider. The thing was entwined in something like a sheet, limp and motionless, and exactly the size of a man.

"Dear God," she whispered with dread. "Dear God, dear God, dear God." It was a prayer, the only one she was capable of forming.

She started to go forward. She stepped off the porch, then her legs suddenly became like lead. She could not move; she was frozen there, helpless and horrified.

He came to her and slowly dismounted. He looked atrocious. But it was not upon her nephew that her own eyes were riveted, but on the shrouded body flung over his horse.

"He told you," Hakon said, "that he would come home."

She took a deep breath and fought down the fury which suddenly swelled up inside her. She ripped her gaze away from her son and steadily faced his murderer. For a long and wild and terrible moment the widow of Erlend was sure she herself would kill.

Then a voice cried in her heart, *No! No!* The dead son draped over that horse would be the last to ever condone his mother's murderous rage. She must not give in!

Then, in a flash, she remembered her little boy inside the house, and his gentle Papa with him, and how they were both asleep and defenseless. Whatever violence had passed yesterday between Magnus and this her nephew, she did not know, nor what horrors she would see if she later unwrapped that shroud. But one thing she did know was that the man standing before her was now the sole Orkney Jarl and carried the power to do whatsoever he chose to her family inside. She realized instantly that she was entirely at the mercy of this monster.

Falling to her knees at his feet, the mother of Magnus implored, "Please, my Lord Jarl! Do not harm us! I beg thee, in the name of God!"

To her amazement, all her nephew said was, "Get up. Take your son and bury him where you will."

Trembling she rose from her knees and stood silent before her Jarl, a fire still raging in her heart, as twilight settled slowly over Paplay. She had promised herself earlier that she would cling to those words of Magnus with all her might and main, and she had to do it quickly before hatred overcame her. *Both* had forgiven this animal! Not just her saintly Magnus, dead here before her, but even her hot-blooded and vengeful Aerling as well. Could the woman who bore them dishonor the brave sons of Erlend by refusing to do the same?

Lady Thora wiped away the unshed tears which burned her eyes. She looked back one last time at the remains of the child she had so loved, with those huge stains of blood seeped through one end of the winding sheet, and her battle was suddenly won. Holding out her arms to her nephew, she said, "I would be to thee, my lord, as a mother. Be to me a son. That is all I ask of thee from hence."

She saw her nephew shut his eyes with despair and lean, exhausted, against his horse with its burden. Then he hid his face in his hands and bitterly wept.

Afterword

Through the intercession, no doubt, of his cousin Saint Magnus, Hakon Paalson repented of his terrible crime. He traveled for some time as a pilgrim in the Holy Land, trying his best to atone for his sin, and was absolved by none less than the Pope himself. Hakon died a few short years later, having reigned briefly as the sole Orkney Jarl. His two sons, Paal and Harald, ascended the throne after him.

Eventually, as time went on, Kol Kalison urged his son Rognavald to sail west to the Orkneys and lay claim to his half of the kingdom, being the eldest surviving male on the side of Erlend, and thus one of the rightful heirs. Accepting his father's advice, the great-grandson of Thorfinn the Mighty made a vow to his sainted uncle, promising to build a magnificent cathedral in his honor if Magnus would aid him from Heaven in his bold endeavor. Confident that his prayer would be heard, Saint Magnus's young nephew Rognavald, together with Kol, left the shores of their home in Norway and headed to war against the sons of Hakon.

But the story of Saint Rognavald is its own tale, and deserving of its own telling . . .